MANAGING
POLICE ORGANIZATIONS

edited by

GARY W. CORDNER
Eastern Kentucky University

DENNIS J. KENNEY
Police Executive Research Forum

anderson publishing co.
p.o. box 1576
cincinnati, oh 45201-1576

Selected Articles from the American Journal of Police

Managing Police Organizations

ISBN 0-87084-142-4
Library of Congress Catalog Number 95-75512

The text of this book is printed on recycled paper.

Cover design by Marnie Deacon.

Table of Contents

Preface

Police organizations are challenging to manage. The police manager, first of all, has to maintain both an internal perspective and an external perspective. The internal perspective focuses on the organization itself, while the external perspective focuses on the world around the organization.

The internal perspective of police management involves such activities as creating the structure of the organization, designing strategies and programs, acquiring staff and other resources, and managing people. Basically, this internal perspective is focused on running the organization—on figuring out what the organization and its personnel should do and then seeing that it gets done. Key processes include planning, decisionmaking, and implementation.

This description makes the internal dimension of police management seem simpler and more straightforward than it really is, though. For example, in order to figure out what the organization should do, police managers need to know with some degree of consensus and precision (1) what the organization is supposed to accomplish (its ends), (2) what options are available (its means), and (3) the consequences of different options. In reality, of course, the ends of policing are multiple, vague, and sometimes controversial; there is often more disagreement than consensus over them. Furthermore, the body of reliable knowledge about the means of policing, and particularly about the consequences or effects of different alternatives, is decidedly skimpy and immature. Therefore, when trying to chart their organization's course, police managers frequently do not know quite where they are supposed to go nor how to get there. One result of this predicament is that the practice of police administration is often more reactive, cautious, and crisis-oriented than we might hope.

Similarly, managing people within police organizations is trickier than one might think. For one thing, the stakes are very high—police officers have awesome authority and lethal weapons, so tight controls over some kinds of actions and decisions are expected. At the same time, though, police officers are granted wide discretion in many matters and usually perform their jobs out of sight of supervisors and managers. Police officers also experience danger, hostility, isolation, and stress, conditions that sometimes affect officers' values, personalities, and health. Thus, police managers are in charge of employees who work in very volatile circumstances with extensive authority, wide discretion, and little immediate supervision—it is not surprising that these managers often seem a bit nervous themselves and quite concerned about the adequacy of their liability insurance coverage.

As if the dilemmas and demands inherent in the internal dimension of police management were not sufficiently challenging, the external dimension is perhaps even more complex and intense. This aspect of police management is concerned with the police organization's environment; responsibilities include acquiring resources, fending off threats, and taking advantage of opportunities. In general, managers must monitor the environment to ensure the organization's survival and adaptation to changing conditions. They can also sometimes fill a more proactive role by influencing the environment to change in ways that are beneficial to the organization.

The environment of the police organization contains a host of significant actors and interest groups, including politicians, other government agencies, the courts, the media, labor unions, police professional associations, business leaders, community groups, and individual citizens. These groups interact with police organizations in different ways: they demand services or information, impose regulations, provide resources or information, or sit in judgment of police actions. Police interactions with these groups can run the gamut from active collaboration and cooperation through peaceful coexistence to outright conflict. The manager's responsibility is to ensure that the interactions benefit the police organization and, in the long run, contribute to the attainment of society's goals and objectives for policing.

This volume on *Managing Police Organizations* contains ten recent articles from the *American Journal of Police* that focus primarily on either the external dimension of police management or on the more strategic and planning-oriented aspects of the internal dimension. A companion volume, *Managing Police Personnel,* focuses more on those aspects of the internal dimension pertinent to managing people.

The articles in this volume are organized in three sections. The first, "The Context of Police Management," presents articles on politics, labor relations, civilian review, and police-minority relations. The second section, "Legal and Policy Issues," addresses the impact of civil liability, Supreme Court decisions, and administrative rule-making on police organizations. The final section, "Performance and

Accountability," contains articles on measuring police performance, ethics, and future demographic influences on police administration.

These articles, written by some of today's leading police authorities, raise important issues, present careful analyses, and suggest promising directions for improving both policing and police management. As editors of the *American Journal of Police*, we were pleased to see these articles first published in the journal and are even more pleased to be able to present them in one package for the benefit of students and practitioners of police management.

Section I

The Context of Police Management

Introduction

This section contains articles focused on four interesting and challenging issues facing police organizations and police managers: (1) the influence of politics on police executives; (2) collective bargaining and labor relations; (3) external or "civilian" review of complaints against the police; and (4) the role of police leaders in addressing police-minority relations. Each of these articles discusses the background of its topical issue and also presents some fresh information that helps us understand the issue a little better. The first three articles present cross-sectional data with some quantitative analysis (higher math not required). The fourth article is in the form of a case study using more qualitative methods.

In the article "Political Pressures and Influences on Police Executives," Ken Tunnell and Larry Gaines present findings from a survey of Kentucky police chiefs. Their findings confirm much of the conventional wisdom about the tenuous political positions of police executives. The chiefs who were surveyed in 1989, for example, reported that over 50% of their predecessors had been forced out of office by political superiors. During 1990, following the 1989 election year, 24% of the state's police chiefs left their jobs. In such turbulent situations, with the fear of being fired or demoted so ever-present, it is not surprising that many chiefs manage their organizations very cautiously.

The chiefs surveyed by Tunnell and Gaines were also asked to identify the types and sources of political pressure that they had experienced. While a majority reported that they had encountered political pressure of some kind, most thought they were better off than their predecessors. Mayors and city council members were identified as the main sources of pressure; little pressure from business leaders or state politicians was cited. The greatest amount of pressure pertained to arrest/enforcement decisions and special services, while the least was felt in the area of promotions. The extent of political pressure exerted on the chiefs varied greatly between jurisdictions, but no consistent differences by agency size were found.

David Carter and Al Sapp used a national survey of medium and large police departments (those with 100+ sworn personnel) to obtain 328 collective bargaining agreements as a means of studying one of the most vexing aspects of police administration—labor relations. They analyzed the contents of these agreements and compared their findings to those from a similar study conducted ten years earlier. They found that the agreements had changed considerably over the decade, with no clear-cut winner between labor and management. Apparently, though, both sides had grown more sophisticated in labor relations, perhaps to the public's benefit.

Some of Carter's and Sapp's findings are quite interesting. The collective bargaining agreements generally had become less restrictive of management in such areas as management rights clauses, maintenance of standards and benefits language, promotion, and assignment. Labor had made gains with respect to grievances, disciplinary procedures, layoffs, and recalls. One of the most dramatic changes was a reduction in automatic cost of living adjustments. The authors conclude that "the police collective bargaining process is stabilizing. Management's seat at the bargaining table is increasingly one of true negotiation rather than reaction."

In "The Effectiveness of Civilian Review," Sam Walker and Vic Bumphus report a surprising recent development: civilian review is back in a big way. Nearly extinct by the early 1970s, and always controversial among police personnel, civilian review "boards" can now be found in two-thirds of the 50 largest U.S. cities. "Boards" is within quotation marks because civilian review procedures were found to vary considerably among the different cities, in some cases constituting an individual or an agency rather than a multi-member committee or board.

Walker and Bumphus point out that we presently lack "any independent evaluations of the effectiveness of any [civilian review] procedure, much less any comparative studies." They carefully identify some of the impediments to documenting and comparing the effectiveness of civilian review systems, in particular the ambiguity of official data. At the end of their article, they issue a call for more careful descriptions, evaluations, and comparisons of civilian review procedures so that at some future point we will have a better answer to the question "what works?"

In "Police Leadership and the Reconciliation of Police-Minority Relations," Ken Betsalel presents a readable and convincing case study of one noted police executive—former San Jose Police Chief Joseph McNamara. The focus of the article is on McNamara's apparently successful effort to redefine the terms of his police department's relations with its minority community. This effort is particularly significant since much of the conflict between American police departments and their environments over at least the last 30 years has occurred within the realm of police-community relations, a code phrase in most jurisdictions for police-minority relations, and especially for police relations with the African American community.

To Betsalel, the key feature of McNamara's approach was his adoption of "transforming" or "moral" leadership:

> the kind of leadership that does not eliminate the complex conflicts inherent in the value demands of democracy and bureaucracy but instead attempts to teach the kind of moral strength and reliance on the rule of law that over time will empower both police and minority citizens to reconcile those competing value claims for themselves.

We'll leave it to you to discover how Chief McNamara exemplified such transformational and moral leadership.

Political Pressures and Influences on Police Executives: A Descriptive Analysis

Kenneth D. Tunnell
Eastern Kentucky University

Larry K. Gaines
Eastern Kentucky University

The purpose of this study was to examine the degree of political interference or pressure exerted on police chief executives by public and private officials, the location or areas of political interference, and their impact on police executives. Additionally, we examined the level and source of pressure on predecessor chiefs and the predecessors' longevity to determine average tenure of police chiefs.

Although scant, the literature, relative to political interference on police chiefs by public and private officials, has developed accordingly: the political nature of local government; the process of becoming a police chief; the effects of community structure and values on police organizations; and the relationship between political officials and police executives. Informed by this literature, we collected and analyzed survey data from Kentucky police chiefs relative to the political processes and pressures that they experience. The findings from this research speak to the quality and quantity of political interference on police chiefs by public and private officials.

Police Executives and the Political Process

Because official government is the nucleus of both politics and political activities in our society, it follows that the police—the component of government that wields legitimate force—and how they are managed, are influenced by and through various political processes. Indeed, this situation has long been recognized by concerned public officials who periodically have attempted to eliminate, or at least reduce, the influence of politics on law enforcement and its potential for corruption. In 1929, for example, President Hoover appointed the National Commission on Law Observance and Enforcement to study police problems. As a result, a variety of state and local commissions, such as those in New York City across the years, have examined the problems resulting from politics and policing (e.g., Fogelson, 1977).

The National Commission on Law Observance and Enforcement (1931) found that partisan politics played a key role in police corruption, police inefficiency, and the use of police as pawns to supplant community interests for those of politicians. The political reigns on police departments prevented them from effectively performing the critical functions that the citizenry expected of them. The Commission concluded that politics should be absent from policing. Research since the Commission found that numerous citizens believed police in many cases were nothing more than adjuncts to political machines, and that police reform not only improved policing, but also attacked the infrastructure of political machines (Fogelson, 1977).

The effects of politics on police personnel administration historically have been devastating. For example, in 1917 a newly elected Republican Mayor in Louisville, Kentucky dismissed over 300 officers from a force of 429 (Fosdick, 1972). Likewise, in Salt Lake City, police attrition after an election ran as high as 85 percent. And in Indianapolis, politicians attempting to remedy the constant turmoil, dictated that all police ranks be equally divided between Republicans and Democrats. The police chief and everyone in the department were scrutinized by politicians eager to provide political patronage to their supporters and punish their foes.

Given that American law enforcement was dominated by politics and political machines during the early decades of this century, it is astonishing that police chiefs now have any independence. And indeed, some jurisdictions never have been able to dislodge the shackles imposed by political machines. Chicago, for example, arguably is little different today than it was at the turn of the century (e.g., Robinson, 1975).

A contemporary study examined political "interference" or "intrusion" in 24 police departments (Mastrofski, 1988). Numerous factors were discovered that mediate the degree and type of interference exerted on police executives. Some of the most telling included community size, the community's social class, the size of the department, and its dominant values. Furthermore, the study suggested that levels of interference may vary as a result of the personalities of individuals involved in governance, the political culture, the degree of police bureaucratization, and the community power structure (Mastrofski, 1988).

Undoubtedly, politics have not been removed from policing. Although just as prevalent today, political influences are qualitatively different than those during the earlier part of this century. Political influences are much more subtle; they affect policy issues as opposed simply to people and events. They also tend to involve a greater plurality of citizens and interest groups as opposed to political demagoguery (e.g., Mills, 1956; Dahl, 1961; Gilbert, 1967; Manley, 1983). This is not to say that politics have been eliminated from policing, but that the political situation in many jurisdictions is "better" or less intrusive than in years past. For example, many of the conditions found in police departments earlier this century, and detailed in earlier work (e.g., Fosdick, 1972; Fogelson, 1977), are not as prevalent in those same departments today.

One of the most noticeable changes in police administration as a result of political reforms has been the increasing influence of the professional police chief. One facet of this development may be that police chiefs in some locales have more independence than their predecessors. Although a number of policy boundaries or parameters remain, many of today's chiefs have more decisionmaking latitude than their predecessors. Comprehending the subtle differences in executive independence among police chiefs is imperative if police administration is to be thoroughly understood.

Our study sheds light on the political processes of government and business as they interfere with or affect police chiefs. We describe both qualitative and quantitative categories of political interference and how they influence police executive decisionmaking. Police chiefs frequently find themselves in situations where their autonomy is limited by "bounded rationality" (Simon, 1961). That is, they are not always allowed to select and implement their definitions of optimal solutions for the problems confronting their agencies; political boundaries sometimes prohibit such actions. In an effort to clarify the tenuous positions of chiefs in the political arena, we describe the relationships between chiefs and political representatives within government.

The Political Relationship Between Chiefs and Political Officials

Understanding the nature of the relationship between police executives and government officials is fundamental to understanding the nature of political interference and its impact on policing. By illuminating these relationships and the nature of political interference, we situate them within a context of political dynamics.

Although, literature on the relationships between police chiefs and politicians is scarce, early research focused on politicians' dysfunctional interventions into police administration (e.g., O'Brien, 1978). From his study, O'Brien delineates three types of dysfunctional politicians; the misfeasors, the nonfeasors, and the malfeasors. The misfeasors are motivated by their fears of being accused of inefficiency and thus believe it is imperative to be involved in police administrative matters. The nonfeasors are those who stay detached from everyday police matters (i.e., they are "out of the loop") to remain isolated from negative consequences that may result from both enforcement and nonenforcement decisions. Finally, the malfeasors are those who are both corrupt and intent on using their office as a means of manipulating the police for their own benefit. These three types of political officials seldom exist in their purist form.

Regardless of their attitudes or inclinations, police chiefs must work with public officials. Indeed, a former Commissioner of the New York City Police Department and President of the Police Foundation readily concedes that politicians have a legitimate stake in areas such as the prioritization of police problems, the facilitation of media relations, municipal policy making, and the deployment of personnel (Murphy, 1985). He admonished potential police chiefs to negotiate not only the terms of their contracts, but also where ultimate authority in specific police policy areas rests. Andrews (1985:7) likewise supports the notion that relationships should be formally negotiated.

> Without clear bounds of legally established authority, clear day-to-day relationships cannot be established, and consequently much personal and organizational energy must be expended on each issue or event as it develops to define the power and the working and the authority relationships. Such continuing uncertainty does not improve either city government or police organization stability or success.

If relationships are not articulated and understood clearly, not only will a great deal of individual and organizational energy be expended, but ultimately the relations between the police and government officials may strain to the point that the chief is replaced. This is especially poignant in cases where there is a veteran chief and a new city manager is hired, a new mayor is elected, or new council members assume office. Once new public officials assume office, chiefs are advised to develop a plan or course of action to control various aspects of their jobs and to delineate duties and responsibilities (Scott, 1986). Such a plan seemingly would minimize problems between police chiefs and these new officials.

Considerable effort from the police chief and the political official is required for a meaningful working relationship. For example, Regoli et al. (1989a; 1989b) found that the most important factors contributing to police chief job satisfaction were autonomy, job security, salary, and job conditions regardless of department size. However, police chiefs must be mindful that total autonomy is seldom attainable, and that job security, salary, and job conditions are dependent on the relationships forged with governmental leadership. A former Minneapolis Mayor advises that many law enforcement matters require careful planning and cooperation between the chief and executive, and if this cooperation does not exist, both are doomed to failure (Fraser, 1985). And a former Superintendent of Police in Chicago notes that,

> . . . the chief's ability to serve as a major municipal policy maker—and even his ability to run a police department free from the most outrageous kinds of partisan political incursions—is largely dependent on local idiosyncrasies rather than on the scientific application of immutable principles concerning the police chief-mayor relationship (Brzeczek, 1985:55).

It becomes clear then, that even good working relationships may not always shield the police chief or prevent unwholesome interferences into police departments. With this in mind, this research was undertaken to examine political interference in police administration and to understand the relationship between the police executive and governmental officials.

Research Methods

Within the context of this research, political pressure, as a concept, is used to delineate subjective political pressure, as opposed to objective pressure, on the police executive. By subjective pressure, we mean those pressures felt, intuited or perceived (e.g., Blumer, 1969) as opposed to objective pressures representing acts of power performed to alter police executives' decisions or actions. The degree of subjective pressure on police chiefs is predicated on their definitions of such pressures and their magnitude rather than actual events or conditions.

We use subjective interpretations rather than objective pressures since we were interested in the levels of pressures perceived by police executives. For example, a politician or significant other may exert pressure but the recipient may not define it as such, it may be inane, or the police executive may possess sufficient political powers to rebut the pressure. In another example, a politician or significant other may make benign or innocent statements, but due to the existing political environment or the police executive's previous experiences, these statements might be interpreted as an exertion of political pressure. Thus, the subjective interpretations are of interest to us and represent the dependent variable in this study. Similar general terms have been used by other researchers to describe subjective pressure. For example, Mastrofski (1988) examined "political interference" or "intrusion" and Regoli et al. (1990) examined "community influence." In an effort to better understand or place contextual constraints on these interpretations, respondents were asked to report on both the sources of pressures and the areas where pressures were exerted.

The focus of this study was on Kentucky police chiefs. An exhaustive list of chiefs, which represents the most accurate such list available, was obtained from the Kentucky Department of Criminal Justice Training. A questionnaire was constructed and mailed to all municipal and county police chiefs in Kentucky regardless of the size of their departments. Thus, chiefs were mailed a survey whether their department employed one or several dozen officers. A total of 277 questionnaires was mailed with a letter requesting cooperation.. Although we did not mail a follow-up letter and requested that each chief state where he was employed, surprisingly 115 (42%) surveys were returned. Although requesting such information may have negatively affected the response rate, we believe it was necessary to perform jurisdictional-specific comparisons and to determine which chiefs, indeed, lost or quit their jobs after mayoral elections.

The questionnaires were mailed in November 1989 which preceded the mayoral elections across the state. Every four years all mayors in Kentucky are elected and are then free to make political appointments to the office of police chief. This generally results in a significant turnover of police chiefs the following year. We timed the mailing this way to identify the current chiefs before new mayors assumed office. Therefore, the questionnaires were completed by chiefs who were acutely aware of the political limitations on their tenure.

Findings

Police Chief and Departmental Characteristics

Based on the 115 responses from police chiefs, we found that they had held their present position for an average of 5.5 years and that they had been employed with their respective departments an average of 12.1 years. More recent studies indicate that the average tenure of police chiefs range from 5.5 years (Witham, 1985) to 5.68 years (Enter, 1986). However, 23% of the respondents (N=26) had served only one year as police chief, and 64% of the respondents had been chief for five years or less. This finding is similar to national data which report that 50% of police executives have fewer than four years tenure while only 26% have eight years or more (IACP, 1975).

We were interested in whether tenure and political pressure were related. In an effort to investigate this concern, we examined the relationship between the chiefs' tenure and the amount of political pressure they encountered. We found a mild, inverse relationship between tenure and political pressure. Although the direction of the relationship was expected, we anticipated that this relationship would have been stronger than found here ($r = -.136$, $p = .153$).

The police departments represented in our sample averaged 15.8 full-time officers (sd=37.1). There were several larger departments in the sample that skewed this mean. The chiefs in our sample averaged a yearly salary of $20,000 to $25,000. Finally, the respondents served jurisdictions with an average population of 11,184 (ranging from 500 to 230,000).

Perceived Effectiveness of Previous Chiefs

The survey contained questions about predecessor chiefs. These questions were included in an effort to better understand the effectiveness, popularity, and ultimate demise of the former police chief in each jurisdiction. We intuitively believed that current chiefs would have better insights about their predecessors than they would about themselves. We also believed that since the former police chiefs' careers had been completed, details about their careers (especially their cessation) would yield more pertinent information than details of current chiefs.

Table 1 provides data on predecessor police chiefs vacating their positions—data based on the recollections and assertions of current chiefs.

From the current chiefs' recollections, it is clear that their predecessors left under some degree of political pressure. A total of 44% of the predecessor chiefs left their positions as a result of political pressure, and an additional nine percent were demoted. These findings indicate that political pressure contributes significantly to police chief non-survival. An additional 30 chiefs or 26% left for personal reasons.

Although a number of reasons could account for their decision to resign, it is very conceivable that politics may have played a role in some of these cases.

The respondents were asked to rate their predecessors in terms of their performance. They were asked their perceptions of how the communities, governments, and rank-and-file officers would have rated their predecessors' performance. On a Likert scale ranging from one (poor performance) to seven (outstanding performance), the respondents' perceptions were that the rank and file officers would have ranked the predecessor chiefs an average of 3.3; the community an average of 3.6; and the local government an average of 3.1. Hence, the responses indicate that the community, rank-and-file officers, and the government would have rated the previous chief as somewhat less than adequate.

Table 1

Reasons Given for Predecessor Chiefs' Departure from the Department

Reason	Number	Percent
Personal reasons	30	26.5
Retired after successful service	20	17.7
Terminated by the government	20	17.7
Resigned due to political pressure	19	16.8
Retired due to political pressure	11	9.7
Demoted within the department	10	8.8
Died	3	2.7

Finally, the relationships between why their predecessors left their departments and their ratings were examined. The various reasons for leaving the department that related to political pressure and the absence of political pressure were collapsed into a dichotomous variable. Analyses of variance were computed using the rank-and-file ratings, community ratings, and governmental leaders' ratings as the dependent variables. As depicted in Table 2, those chiefs who left for reasons other than political pressure uniformly had significantly higher ratings than did those chiefs who departed under political pressure.

Political Pressures Exerted on Current Chiefs

The police chiefs were asked to provide information about the types of political pressures they presently encounter from the mayor, city council members, local business leaders and state politicians. The respondents were asked specifically to rate the relative amount of political pressure that they encounter in their decisions to (1) hire officers, (2) promote or demote officers, (3) arrest offenders or enforce specific laws, (4) make unnecessary changes in personnel assignments such as transfers to and from specialized units, and (5) provide special or unusual services to individuals or groups within the community. As illustrated in Table 3, the respondents reported that they had some pressure in each of these areas from the mayors and city council members but little from business leaders. The participants reported virtually no pressure from state politicians.

Table 2

Analysis of Variance between the Support of Various Groups and the Pressures of Political Interference in Decisions to Leave the Department

Support Group	F-value	p value
Rank-and-file Police Ratings	7.70	.0069*
Community Ratings	8.79	.0040*
Government Leaders Ratings	24.15	.0001*

* In each instance, those chiefs who left as a result of political pressure had significantly lower ratings than those who left under no pressure.

First, regarding personnel decisions, 21% of the participants reported that their mayors pressured them in decisions to hire or terminate officers and 22% reported that city council members pressured them in this area. Ten percent of the respondents reported some pressure in hiring decisions from business leaders. Also, 16% of the chiefs reported pressure from the mayor in promotion decisions,

16% reported pressure from city council members in this area, and none reported pressure from business leaders in this area. Finally, 23% of the chiefs reported pressure from the mayor in making special personnel assignments, 17% reported this pressure from city council members, and 6% reported that business leaders attempted to influence them in this area. Thus, it appears that personnel decisions are not necessarily autonomous decisions residing within the purview of the chief's authority.

Second, regarding political pressure in police operations, 28% of the chiefs reported pressure from the mayor in arrest or enforcement decisions, 29% reported pressure in arrest and enforcement decisions from city council members, and 6% claimed business leaders attempted to influence their decisions in this area. Twenty-seven percent of the police chiefs reported being asked by mayors to provide unusual or special services, 29% of the chiefs were asked for these services by city council members, and 13% of the chiefs recounted some pressure in this area.

Table 3

Police Chief Self-Reporting on Type and Location of Political Pressure: By Percent

Source	Personnel Decisions	Promotion Decisions	Personnel Assigns.	Arrest & Enforce.	Special Services
Mayor	21.0	15.8	23.0	28.0	27.0
City Council	21.6	16.5	17.1	29.0	29.1
Business Leaders	10.0	0	6.3	6.3	12.6

Thus, it appears that the local politicians have a direct effect on operational decisions in almost one-third of the police agencies.

Third, we conducted further analyses to assess whether political pressure patterns exist. The rating patterns of the mayors and city council members were intercorrelated to determine if similar patterns existed for each. Business leaders and state politicians were not used in the analyses because they were reported to interfere considerably less than mayors and city council members. Again, pressure in the following areas was assessed: (1) hiring and firing officers; (2) promoting and demoting officers; (3) arresting offenders or enforcing specific laws; (4) making unnecessary changes in personnel assignments such as transfers to and from specialized units; and (5) providing special or unusual services to individuals or groups within the community. We generally found that those chiefs who were pressured in one area by the mayors were pressured in other areas by the mayors as evidenced by high correlation coefficients. The intercorrelations among the areas range from a low of $r=.553$ ($p=.0001$) to a high of $r=.739$ ($p=.0001$). Again, these correlations indicate that if a mayor exerted pressure in one area, he or she was likely to in another. Next, the intercorrelations for the city council members were examined, and the range of correlations was from r=.379 (p=.0001) to a high of r=.736 (p=.0001). These significant correlations indicate that officials, when exerting pressure on police chiefs, do so across a wide area rather than only one area. It is also interesting that city council members seemingly exert more pressure than mayors except in personnel assignments, contrary to Mastrofski's (1988) findings that city council members are rarely involved in daily police activities. Perhaps this difference lies in part in the size of jurisdictions. Mastrofski's jurisdictions were much larger than those used here.

Kentucky's cities are classified into six classes based on size. We investigated whether city size had any impact on the political pressure exerted on chiefs. The relationship between city size as measured by the city's class and the amount of self-reported political pressure (a question about general political pressure using a Likert scale) resulted in a correlation coefficient of r=.034, (p=.725). This insignificant correlation indicates that city size has no appreciable effect on the amount of political pressure exerted on chiefs. Thus, it appears that governmental officials, regardless of city size, are equally guilty of this practice.

Finally, the respondents were questioned about general pressure they encounter while performing their jobs as police chief, and 56% reported they encounter political pressure. As alarming as this is, interestingly they believe they are under less pressure than their predecessors. We cannot be certain if they actually experience less pressure than their predecessors, but most importantly, they perceive that they experience less. This may indicate that they believe they are in better control of their political environments and that politics is playing a less important role in policing than in the past. Even so, several respondents volunteered written comments describing the need for better insulation and protection from the politicians and the need for job security, perhaps in the form of civil service protection. The following two comments exemplify the chiefs' desire to have some form of job protection.

- I believe it's time to have some protection for police chiefs from the threat of being fired by some individual, that is the mayor [who] does not agree with the decisions the chief might have to make. We have the policeman's bill of rights and the chiefs should be included in this hearing process before being dismissed by politicians. It's time we stood up for our rights in this matter. (From a 30-year veteran who has been chief for 22 years of a city of 8,000).

- Police chiefs throughout the state need some type of protection to assist them in upgrading old and outdated ways small departments have been run, without fear of losing their jobs. I am appointed on a yearly basis which makes it difficult to stand up for the department, citizens, and very much needed training without fear of not being re-appointed each year. (From a chief who has been with the department three years, two of which as chief. The department has five full-time officers in a town of 6,000 population.)

The following two comments indicate the nature and extent of political pressure placed on police chiefs.

- I need to explain, political interference is different. For example, a council member received a ticket and funding for a new building was blocked, same council member opposes salary increases. Instead of voicing support for police from council members, you get no comment. (From a Chief with a force of 75 officers serving a city of 51,000.)

- In my case, I have consistently been subjected to more pressure from the city manager than from all other sources combined. Obviously, on some occasions, he was speaking for politicians or other community leaders but they were not identified. More often, he was expressing his view on the administration of the police department. (From a chief with 48 officers serving a population of 27,000. He has been chief approximately seven years.)

The following two comments are indicative of the respondents' concerns about the then-approaching mayoral elections and the potential effects on their tenure and autonomy.

- With the current mayor and council, no interference. But with the election next month, we are looking at interference from the new members. (From a chief serving a city of 13,000 population and with less than two years of experience as chief.)

- The current mayor is not seeking re-election. After the election on November 7, I expect every answer on this study to change. (From a chief serving a city of 7,500 with 13 officers. He has been chief for one year and reported little pressure at the time of the study.)

In support of their concerns, the Kentucky Department of Criminal Justice Training reported that 24% (N=66) of Kentucky police chiefs left their jobs during 1990, the year immediately following elections and the new mayors assuming office. Undoubtedly, many of these were either dismissed or demoted.

Conclusions

The data indicate that Kentucky police chiefs must cope with varying levels of political pressures and interference, some legitimate and some illegitimate. Our study, for the most part, agrees with earlier findings. We found political pressures are exerted from a variety of directions, and as a result, over 50% of the police chiefs who had left their jobs in our study were forced out by governmental politicians (see Table 1). We have no measure as to how many of these removals were justified.

What is becoming increasingly clear however, is that we know very little about this political process. The literature abounds with anecdotes on the problems of police executives, but offers little beyond these descriptive illustrations. We must initiate attempts at quantifying, better understanding, and controlling these relationships if policing is truly to become free of political interference. We also realize that this is a double-edged sword. Recent events in Los Angeles point to a problem where the police chief possessed too much autonomy. However, there are numerous other examples where chiefs have been unable to ensure that their departments provided the best possible service because of a lack of political autonomy. As Goldstein (1977) has noted, it is extremely difficult to maintain a working balance between police responsiveness and political accountability. At this point, police administration, at least in Kentucky, is severely bounded by these relationships, which removes a large degree of management discretion from police administrators.

References

Andrews, A. (1985). "Structuring the Political Independence of the Police Chief." *Police Leadership in America: Crisis and Opportunity* W. Geller (ed.). New York: Praeger Press.

Blumer, H. (1969). *Symbolic Interactionism: Perspective and Method.* Englewood Cliffs, NJ: Prentice-Hall.

Brzeczek, R. (1985). "Chief-Mayor Relations: The View from the Chief's Chair." *Police Leadership in America: Crisis and Opportunity* W. Geller (ed.). New York: Praeger Press.

Dahl, R. (1961). *Who Governs?* New Haven: Yale University Press.

Enter, J. (1986). "The Rise to the Top: An Analysis of Police Chief Career Patterns." *Journal of Police Science and Administration,* 14(4):334-346.

Fogelson, R. (1977). *Big-City Police.* Cambridge, MA: Harvard University Press.

Fosdick, R. (1972). *American Police Systems* (Reprint Edition). Montclair, NJ: Patterson Smith.

Fraser, D. (1985). "Politics and Police Leadership: The View from City Hall." *Police Leadership in America: Crisis and Opportunity.* W. Geller, (ed.). New York: Praeger Press.

Gilbert, C. (1967). "Some Trends in Community Politics: A Secondary Analysis of Power Structure Data from 166 Communities." *Social Science Quarterly,* 48:373-381.

Goldstein, H. (1977). *Policing a Free Society.* Cambridge, MA: Ballinger.

IACP Police Chief Executive Committee (1975). *Police Chief Executive.* Washington, D.C.: U.S. Government Printing Office.

Manley, J. (1983). "Neopluralism: A Class Analysis of Pluralism I and II." *American Political Science Review,* 77:368-383.

Mastrofski, S. (1988). "Varieties of Police Governance in Metropolitan America." *Politics and Policy,* 8:12-31.

Mills, C. (1956). *The Power Elite.* New York: Oxford University Press.

Murphy, P. (1985). "The Prospective Chief's Negotiation of Authority with the Mayor." *Police Leadership in America: Crisis and Opportunity.* W. Geller (ed.). New York: Praeger Press.

O'Brien, J. (1978). "The Chief and the Executive: Direction or Political Interference?" *Journal of Police Science and Administration,* 6(2):394-401

Regoli, R., J. Crank and Culbertson, R. (1989a). "The Consequences of Professionalism Among Police Chiefs." *Justice Quarterly,* 6(1):47-67.

———— (1989b). "Police Cynicism, Job Satisfaction, and Work Relations of Police Chiefs: An Assessment of the Influence of Department Size." *Sociological Focus,* 22(3):161-171.

Regoli, R., R. Culbertson, J. Crank and J. Powell (1990). "Career Stage and Cynicism Among Police Chiefs." *Justice Quarterly,* 7(3):593-614.

Robinson, C. (1975). "The Mayor and the Police: The Political Role of the Police." *Police Forces in History.* G. Mosse (ed.). Beverly Hills: Sage.

Scott, M. (1986). *Managing for Success: A Police Chief's Survival Guide.* Washington, D.C.: Police Executive Research Forum.

Simon, H. (1961). *Administrative Behavior.* New York: Macmillan.

Witham, D. (1985). *The American Law Enforcement Chief Executive: A Management Profile.* Washington, D.C.: Police Executive Research Forum.

A Comparative Analysis of Clauses in Police Collective Bargaining Agreements as Indicators of Change in Labor Relations[1]

David L. Carter
Michigan State University

Allen D. Sapp
Central Missouri State University

The character of public sector labor relations appears to be changing. While over the past two decades the presence of unionization appears to be slightly declining in the private sector, the reverse is true with respect to the police and fire services. While change is noticeable based on the experiences of administrators and labor representatives, little empirical analysis has been done to measure and describe the change. The published research available on police labor relations generally tends to be narrow, focusing on specific labor clauses or processes (see Gallagher & Veglahn, 1987; Feuille & Delaney, 1986; Connolly, 1986; Wolkinson, Chelst & Shepard, 1985; Feuille, Delaney & Hendricks, 1985; Delaney & Feuille, 1984; Ayres & Ayres, 1981, Bloom, 1981; Kruger & Jones, 1981; Butler & Ehrenberg, 1981; Juris & Feuille, 1973). Due to constraints in length, it is not feasible to present a traditional literature review in addition to a discussion of the current findings. Thus, the reader is urged to examine the cited sources for further information.

The intent of this article is to provide policy guidance in labor negotiations and arbitrations on issues that commonly appear on the table but for which there is little empirical support. Indeed, police chiefs specifically requested that the Police Executive Research Forum (PERF) conduct this study in order to have a broader information base on which to base negotiation positions.

Police labor organizations at the state and national levels have become increasingly sophisticated in providing bargaining advice and support to local collective bargaining units. Similarly, they have become influential through political activism and have been able to further their agenda through lobbying for passage of legislation that is beneficial to the labor movement. As evidenced by the erosion of management rights and the increase in concessions earned by labor organizations, police management has not been as successful on matters of political activism (Sapp, Carter & Stephens, 1990). The need for comprehensive information on issues and trends in police labor relations is paramount for law enforcement executives to enter the bargaining and arbitration processes in the most informed manner. Such information will aid in citing precedent and trends during the negotiation processes, particularly in cases of binding arbitration.[2]

Understanding the nature of change can provide insights for planning and give a glimpse of the future. The analyses presented in this paper are assessments of indicators guided toward this end. Far too little data is available to permit suggesting firm trends that may continue for the next decade. In all likelihood, given changes in the political and economic environments and the maturation of the police labor movement, changes over the next ten years will not be as pronounced as in the past decade. Nonetheless, the indicators provide important insights in planning for negotiations.

In 1981 the Police Executive Research Forum (PERF) and the National League of Cities jointly sponsored a comprehensive comparative analysis of critical clauses in police collective bargaining agreements (CBAs) (Rynecki & Morse, 1981). That study established the first comprehensively known standard of negotiated CBA provisions in law enforcement. With change in the police labor environment, "not to mention factors such as educational issues, health care, disciplinary processes and grievances-the need for an update of this benchmark research became apparent. At the urging of police executives who wanted updated information, PERF sought to reexamine the issues and expand the Rynecki and Morse study.

Method

This paper focuses on only one aspect of the complete labor relations study. Presented are the results of a detailed content analysis of 328 police collective bargaining agreements (or memoranda of understanding) as compared to the findings of Rynecki and Morse (1981). A questionnaire was mailed to the chief executives of all U.S. municipal, county, consolidated and primary state law enforcement agencies serving populations of 50,000 or more or having 100 or more sworn officers, a total of 699 agencies. A response rate of 83.7 percent was received from the population with 585 agencies returning completed surveys. Of that total, 323 (55.2%) reported having a current CBA with one or more groups of sworn employees. This group of agencies returned a total of 328 current collective bargaining agreements, contracts, and memoranda or letters of agreement.[3] A content analysis of the 328 CBAs was performed with provisions of the agreements classified into 62 different types of collective bargaining clauses. The clauses were related to various management prerogatives, compensation and benefit issues, discipline, and similar commonly negotiated factors. Further analysis resulted in a total of 187 research variables in the content analyses. The clauses and variables reported in this paper are those directly comparable to the ones discussed by Rynecki and Morse (1981).

Content analysis is the systematic study of written communication that lends itself to quantitative measures of frequencies of responses. This study focuses on the *manifest content* of information within the agreements. Manifest content, according to Babbie (1992), is the visible content of communication, and not the implied meanings documents may have that the researcher must interpret. Therefore, each clause analyzed had specific written language applicable to this study and no interpretation regarding the spirit of provisions beyond the contract language was made by the researchers. Rather, the researchers' analytic commentary focuses on collective findings and implied changes in the contractual provisions over the decade.

For comparability, the definitions and the classifications used in the content analyses of this study are the same used by Rynecki and Morse. Inherent in the analytic methodology was a five-tier classification scheme to generally address legal and regulatory environments in which the CBAs were negotiated. The typology, or more specifically, the operational definitions for the types of clauses employed in both studies, is as follows:

Type I Contracts with strong clauses listing extensive rights that are not grievable.

Type II Contracts with comprehensive clauses which imply that use of rights may be grievable.

Type III Contracts with specific clauses listing fewer rights and implying their use may be grievable.

Type IV Contracts using residual rights.

Type V Contracts specifically stating that management rights may be subject to grievances or negotiation (Rynecki & Morse, 1981:8).

The five types of clauses ranged from the strongest to the weakest in terms of establishing management's rights to conduct the affairs of the agency as defined above. These operational definitions of clauses, while somewhat subjective, are actually fairly easy to apply to contract analysis given the usual precision in contract language. As a point of nomenclature, for purposes of readability, the authors use *collective bargaining agreement* as a collective term to include the more formal labor contracts and the less formal memoranda of understanding.

Rynecki and Morse (1981) had 140 collective bargaining agreements in their study while the current research includes 328. Because the earlier study's results were reported in proportions and the N-sizes were larger than thirty, the Z-Test for differences between proportions was used to test the significance of observed differences between the two studies. Moreover, since both studies used nearly the same population (without sampling) and the results are tested in proportions, the comparability is generally controlled despite differences in N-sizes between the two studies (Leonard, 1976).[4] Use of these analytic methods provides policy information on changes in the collective bargaining experience of the nation's largest law enforcement agencies, information that can be used in the contract planning and negotiation processes.

Results

Management Rights Clauses

The term management rights as used in collective bargaining pertains to language that provides for authority of management to carry out the function of the department and to manage that function. In analyzing management right clauses, Rynecki and Morse (1981) used the five-tier operational definitions previously described.

There was no change in the proportion of collective bargaining agreements with Type I clauses. Each study found ten percent of the contracts in which extensive rights are assigned to management that cannot be grieved. The number of CBAs with no mention or language about management rights increased from 11 percent in 1981 to 16 percent in 1990. This difference in proportions was not statistically significant. The data in Table 1 provide comparisons of the two PERF studies.

Table 1
Management Rights Clauses

Type Clause	1981	1991	% Change	Significance
I (Strongest)	10%	10%	0	n.s.
II (Comprehensive)	14%	27%	+13	$z = 3.401$ $p<.001$
III (General)	32%	31%	–1	n.s.
IV (Residual rights)	11%	14%	+3	n.s.
V (Weakest)	12%	2%	–10	$z = 3.505$ $p<.001$
No language	11%	16%	+5	n.s.

One major shift was noted in the distribution of the types of rights between the 1981 and the 1991 studies. The shift took place in Type II clauses with comprehensive language concerning management rights, but with the implication that those rights might be grieved. In 1981, 14 percent of the contracts studied contained a Type II clause while in 1991 that proportion had nearly doubled to 27 percent ($z=3.401$, $p<.001$). The gain in Type II clauses came mostly from a reduction of Type V, the weakest type of management rights. The Type V clause, specifically stating that management rights can be grieved or negotiated, dropped from 12 percent in 1981 to only two percent in 1991 ($z=3.505$, $p<.001$). These changes support the notion that police management has increased the sophistication and impact of their negotiations at the expense of the labor groups.

Maintenance of Standards and Benefits

Maintenance of standards and benefits clauses are those that contain language that protects the benefits and standards that existed before the newly negotiated contract.[5] These clauses may also contain language that provides for procedures to effect changes in those existing benefits or standards. The latter language may apply broadly to all such benefits and standards or may be limited to specified topics.

Collectively, in the 1981 study approximately 59 percent of the contracts studied mentioned maintenance of standards or benefits. By the 1991 study, that proportion without maintenance of benefits and standards language had decreased to 33 percent. As noted in Table 2, most of those changes were statistically significant. At first blush, it may appear that the reduction of CBAs with this clause may be an indicator of increased retention of management prerogatives. However, there may be a more likely explanation.

Table 2
Maintenance of Standards and Benefits

Type Clause	1981	1991	% Change	Significance
Prohibits Change	29%	8%	–21	$z = 5.101$ $p<.0001$
Requires Consultation	4%	1%	–3	$z = 3.505$ $p<.001$
Requires Notification	4%	1%	–3	n.s.
Limited Applicability	10%	1%	–9	$z = 3.469$ $p<.001$
Other Language	12%	22%	+10	$z=2.798$ $p<.01$
No language	46%	67%	+21	$z = 4.244$ $p<.0001$

Most CBAs are negotiated for a three-year period. In the late 1970s and early 1980s there was a notable increase in the number of first-time police CBAs (Sapp, Carter & Stephens, 1990; Carter & Sapp, 1992a). The first-time agreements are the ones most likely to have a maintenance of standards and benefits clause. Each successive agreement will address the standards and benefits at issue as negotiated points in the agreement. As these issues are resolved "particularly after two or three iterations of CBAs" the need for a maintenance of standards and benefits clause is reduced (or eliminated). As a result, the significant changes in these clauses most likely represent stable benefits for the collective bargaining groups and a reduction in management prerogatives.

Definitions of Grievances

One of the more important clauses in any CBA is the one defining a grievance and specifying issues which are subject to a grievance. If grievances are narrowly defined and restricted to topics covered in the collective bargaining agreement, the number and type of subsequent grievances are also restricted. Broad definitions of grievances permit the grieving of virtually any management action or decision. In a previous study of law enforcement collective bargaining grievance procedures, a relationship between the definition of grievance and grievance resolution procedures was reported (Sapp, 1980). The narrower definitions were found with more extensive use of arbitration. Very broad definitions were rarely coupled with arbitration.

Rynecki and Morse classified grievance definitions into categories of narrow, limited, and broad. Narrow definitions were those that specified limited grievance issues. In the 1981 study, sixteen percent of the clauses were classified as having a narrow grievance definition. In the current study, only four percent fell into that category. As shown in Table 3, the decrease in the narrowly defined grievance language was statistically significant ($z=2.176$, $p<.05$).

Table 3
Definitions of Grievances

Type Clause	1981	1991	% Change	Significance
Narrow Definition	16%	4%	–12	$z = 2.176$ $p<.05$
Limited Definition	42%	71%	+29	$z = 3.905$ $p<.0001$
Broad Definition	30%	14%	–16	$z = 3.703$ $p<.0001$
None	11%	11%	0	n.s.

Limited definitions were those that defined grievances as restricted to issues directly related to the terms and conditions of the collective bargaining agreement. This has the effect of constraining the types of issues or circumstances that may be subject to the grievance process. Limited definitions of grievances were found in about 42 percent of the 1981 contracts and in 71 percent of the 1991 contracts (z=3.905, p<.0001).

The broad definition category encompassed contracts that permitted issues beyond the scope of the contract to be grieved, including personnel actions and departmental rules and regulations. Broad grievance definitions were noted in 30 percent of the 1981 agreements and in significantly fewer (14 percent) of the 1991 contracts (z=3.703, p<.0001). The implications from these findings are that CBAs are becoming increasingly sophisticated, as is the codification of police department policies, procedures and rules. These changes are positive for management and labor in that discretion and procedural controls are more closely balanced.

Grievance Resolution

Another important issue in collective bargaining centers on the procedures for resolution of grievances. Following the methods used by Rynecki and Morse, the contracts in the current study were classified into three levels of grievance resolution. The least common method of grievance resolution in both studies was the restriction of resolution to internal review within the department (Table 4). Internal resolution was noted in nine percent of the contracts in the earlier research and two percent of the 1991 contracts—a statistically significant change (z=2.905, p<.0001). Some contracts provided for resolution of grievances outside the department but within local government. The proportion of contracts with local government resolution of grievances declined from 12 percent in 1981 to eight percent in 1991.

Table 4
Grievance Resolution

Type Clause	1981	1991	% Change	Significance
Resolved Internally	9%	2%	–7	z = 2.905 p<.01
Resolved in Local Gov't	12%	8%	–4	n.s.
Resolved by Arbitration	92%	83%	–9	z=2.911 p<.01
Binding Arbitration	79%	76%	–3	n.s.
Advisory Arbitration	13%	6%	–7	z = 2.236 p<.05

There was also a decrease in the proportion of agreements that relied on arbitration for grievance resolution. In the earlier study, Rynecki and Morse reported that 92 percent of the contracts provided for arbitration. In the 1991 research, that percentage decreased to 83 percent ($z=2.911$, $p<.01$). Binding arbitration was the form of arbitration used in 79 percent of the contracts in 1981 and in 76 percent in 1991. Advisory arbitration was reported in 13 percent of the contracts in 1981 but in only six percent in 1991 ($z=2.236$, $p<.05$).

As is apparent, some form of arbitration is the most prevalent manner of resolving grievances. The high proportion of CBAs reflecting both binding and non-binding arbitration is a product of multiple provisions in the various agreements which provided a different type of arbitration for different issues that may be grieved. Interestingly, it appears from the authors' research, that the changes found in grievance resolution were externally generated rather than being a product of negotiation per se. Specifically, as a result of state laws defining circumstances in which binding arbitration will be used, precedent established in arbitration proceedings, and decisions from court cases, the need for contractual specifications was reduced.

Disciplinary/Internal Affairs Procedures

In 1981 Rynecki and Morse found that approximately 55 percent of the police CBAs contained a clause with the police officer's Bill of Rights. The current study found only 24 percent of the contracts with the Bill of Rights. That difference was statistically significant ($z= 4.820$, $p<.0001$). An important explanation for this is that nineteen states have enacted laws mandating a police officer Bill of Rights. Not surprisingly, these were the states with the greatest proportion of public safety collective bargaining associations.[6] There were notable differences in the language of contracts dealing with disciplinary actions.

Those clauses providing for disciplinary procedures that are neither subject to review nor reversible by arbitration procedures accounted for 43 percent of the 1981 contracts and 10 percent of the 1991 agreements ($z=7.333$, $p<.0001$, Table 5). Those disciplinary procedures that are reviewed through the contract's grievance and arbitration procedures increased from 24 percent to 37 percent in 1991 ($z=2.897$, $p<.01$). Language in the contracts that permitted the employee to choose a review forum for disciplinary actions declined from 25 percent in 1981 to five percent in the current research ($z=5.404$, $p<.0001$). The most significant change came in those contracts not containing specific provisions for appeal of disciplinary actions. Nine percent of the contracts in 1981 lacked such language but by 1991 that proportion had increased to 48 percent ($z=10.63$, $p<.0001$). Clearly, the review process in disciplinary cases has become increasingly formalized with a defined trend toward delineation of review procedures in the CBA's provisions. This is an important indicator of a reduction in management prerogatives.

Table 5
Disciplinary/Internal Affairs Procedures

Type Clause	1981	1991	% Change	Significance
Not Subject to Review	43%	10%	–33	z = 7.333 p<.0001
Review via CBA Clauses	24%	37%	+13	z = 2.897 p<.01
Right to Choose Forum	25%	5%	–20	z = 5.404 p<.0001
No Appeal Clause	9%	48%	+39	z = 10.63 p<.0001

Civil Service and Third Party Entities

Many states have statutes that establish third-party entities with some authority over police personnel actions and collective bargaining. These entities include state and local civil service commissions, merit boards, fire and police commissions, personnel boards, and labor relations commissions or boards. Often the authority and powers of these entities conflict or overlap in areas normally included within the scope of collective bargaining agreements. To resolve these conflicts, many contracts contain language specifically referring to such entities. Such language may be found in a variety of clauses within the agreement. Collectively, references to civil service or other third-party entities were found in 89 percent of the agreements in both the current research and the Rynecki and Morse study. The distribution of that percentage varied, however, as shown in Table 6.

Table 6
Civil Service and Third-Party Entities

Type Clause	1981	1991	% Change	Significance
Type I	34%	25%	–9	n.s.
Type II	8%	14%	+6	n.s.
Type III	12%	1%	–11	z= 3.385 p<.0001
Type IV	11%	25%	+14	z= 3.927 p<.0001
Type V	24%	24%	0	n.s.
None	16%	11%	–5	n.s.

Attempts to further classify or categorize the references to civil service and other third-party entities could not be done reliably due to the widely varying language used to reflect the authority and limits of the entities.

Type I clauses, those preserving the authority of the other entities, decreased slightly, from 34 percent in 1981 to 25 percent in 1991. Conversely, Type II clauses, those limiting the jurisdiction of third-party entities, increased from eight to 14 percent. Statistically significant changes were noted in Type III and IV clauses. Type III, offering an election to the employee in discipline cases, decreased from 12 percent to one percent ($z=3.385$, $p<.0001$). In Type IV clauses, those allowing employees an option in other than discipline issues, rose from 11 percent in 1981 to 25 percent in 1991 ($z=3.927$, $p<.0001$). The proportion of contracts with Type V clauses, those mentioning the third parties but not describing any jurisdiction for them, remained constant at 24 percent in each study. These findings reinforce the data previously presented, particularly that dealing with grievance resolution.

Staffing Requirements

Language in collective bargaining agreements about staffing requirements typically address the rights of management to establish and maintain levels of staffing (including allocation, deployment and assignment) for individual units or the department. Management seeks to maintain unlimited rights on staffing alternatives while labor often seeks to provide for minimum staffing levels of various units, work conditions or assignments. For example, management seeks to have the flexibility to reassign patrol officers between shifts, days and geography based upon defined service demands as they vary throughout the year. Conversely, labor prefers a defined process for making these assignments which is fixed and not variable unless the change is initiated by the officer. Obviously, compromise is necessary.

Rynecki and Morse found that 61 percent of the contracts contained some language pertaining to staffing requirements. In the current research that proportion had increased to 73 percent. Several changes have taken place. Contracts providing for full management rights in determining staffing requirements increased from 36 percent in 1981 to 42 percent in the latest study (Table 7).

Table 7
Staffing Requirements

Type Clause	1981	1991	% Change	Significance
Full Management Right	36%	42%	+6	n.s.
Implied Management Right	21%	30%	+9	$z = 2.106$ $p<.05$
Other Language	4%	1%	–3	n.s.
No Language	32%	27%	–5	n.s.

Contracts with language implying that management had the right to establish and change staffing requirements increased significantly from 21 percent to 30 percent by 1991(z=2.106, p<.05). The number of contracts containing other language about staffing requirements dropped from four percent in 1981 to one percent in the latest research. Clearly this is a desirable change from management's perspective as it represents a partial restoration of management prerogatives.

Layoffs and Recalls

Major changes have taken place in the language of police CBA clauses in the areas of layoffs, recalls, and reductions in force. The earlier research found that 74 percent of the agreements contained some language dealing with these topics (26 percent had no language). The current project identified 84 percent with such language showing a statistically significant increase (z=2.367, p<.01, Table 8).

Many of the contracts had multiple provisions related to layoffs and recalls. Rynecki and Morse found that one-third (33 percent) of their contracts listed specific circumstances that justified a layoff. The 1991 analysis indicated specified circumstances for layoffs in only five percent of the CBAs (z=6.743, p<.0001). Contracts treating layoffs as a management right without further restrictions decreased over the period between the two studies from 26 percent in 1981 to 11 percent in 1991 (z=3.667, p<.001).

Table 8
Layoffs and Recalls

Type Clause	1981	1991	% Change	Significance
Specified Circumstances	33%	5%	–28	z = 6.743 p<.0001
Management Right	26%	11%	–15	z = 3.667 p<.0001
Standard of Necessity	9%	21%	+12	z = 3.633 p<.001
Exclusive Seniority	35%	40%	+5	n.s.
Seniority as a Factor	4%	6%	+2	n.s.
No Language	26%	16%	–10	z = 2.367 p<.01

The decrease in specified management rights to layoff officers was largely absorbed in language that based layoffs under a standard of necessity that increased significantly from nine percent to 21 percent by 1991 (z=3.633, p<.001). "Standard of necessity" language is often vague and simply notes the right of management to lay off personnel "when necessary"—a circumstance generally meaning that there is fiscal exigency.

In delineating the order of layoffs and recalls, two common examples of language were found in the police collective bargaining agreements. Some contracts, accounting for 35 percent in the earlier study, contained language that specified seniority as the sole criteria in the order of layoffs and recalls. By 1991, that language was found in 40 percent of the contracts. Agreements containing language that specified seniority as a factor in determining the order of layoff and recall increased from four to six percent from between the studies. The differences noted in the use of seniority were not statistically significant but may reflect a developing trend. As seniority becomes less important in other areas of policing (such as promotions and specialized assignments), layoffs and recalls may become the last area where seniority is of importance. Certainly management would interpret the changes in provisions related to recalls and layoffs as another element of restored management prerogatives. It appears that this, along with the increased flexibility in staffing, has been gained by conceding increased benefits in exchange for this flexibility.

Subcontracting

Generally the term "subcontracting" is used in collective bargaining referring to the practice of hiring someone outside the bargaining unit to perform a duty or task that otherwise would be performed by members of the unit. In law enforcement collective bargaining, the term is most frequently applied to the hiring of non-sworn personnel to fill positions formerly held by sworn officers. The practice may also include the use of reserve, auxiliary or volunteers to perform functions that were previously the sole province of the full-time sworn officer. In many agencies this practice has been a volatile issue. Labor groups often oppose subcontracting because it may reduce the number of sworn officers or eliminate sworn officer desk jobs.

When the 1981 study was performed, 63 percent of the contracts mentioned subcontracting. As shown in Table 9, the 1991 study found only 34 percent of the contracts with language concerning subcontracting ($z=5.983$, $p<.0001$). The provisions of most contracts typically addressed management's right to subcontract (rather than the union's position of limiting the practice). This notable change in language was most likely the result of a trend emerging in the 1980s to civilianize the police. That is, police departments began looking at their organizations and found sworn officers in positions such as dispatchers, crime laboratory analysts, researchers, jailers, records clerks, and so forth. Police administrators began to question the wisdom of assigning police officers to duties where no law enforcement authority was needed. It was felt that relieving officers from these positions and replacing them with non-sworn personnel would be more efficient and more effective.

This trend was disturbing to many in police labor organizations because frequently these jobs were viewed as good duty—generally meaning they were on a fixed schedule. This issue became a significant topic of negotiation with management generally winning by broadening its ability to subcontract. An important argument used by management in its negotiation of this issue was that by subcontracting, sworn personnel were in a more solid position should fiscal exigency occur. Moreover, management tended to assure the labor groups that sworn positions would not be lost with increased subcontracting, rather the positions would simply be reassigned.

The language provisions concerned with subcontracting can be classified in three levels of management rights. In 27 percent of the 1981 agreements, management was specifically granted substantive management rights. The current study found statements of substantive management rights in only one percent of the agreements (a significant decrease, $z=5.030$, $p<.0001$). This change means that management had greater breadth in making subcontracting decisions, rather than specified (limited) circumstances or conditions when subcontracting could be used.

Table 9
Subcontracting

Type Clause	1981	1991	% Change	Significance
Substantive Mgmt Right	27%	1%	–26	$z = 5.030$ $p<.0001$
Implied Mgmt Right	30%	20%	–10	$z = 2.243$ $p<.05$
General Rights	7%	13%	+6	$z = 2.108$ $p<.05$
No Language	37%	66%	+29	$z = 5.983$ $p<.0001$

A second category of management rights associated with subcontracting clauses involved language that implied the right of management to subcontract (provisions that are broader than the substantive management rights). In the earlier study, an implied management right to subcontract was found in 30 percent of the agreements. Reflecting the overall decrease in such language, the current study found implied rights in 20 percent of the contracts. This decrease was also statistically significant ($z=2.243$, $p<.05$).

The third category of subcontracting classifications involved statements in the collective bargaining agreement that listed general rights of management to conduct the overall operations of the department. This broad statement of rights was found in seven percent of the CBAs in the previous study and in 13 percent of the current contracts ($z=2.108$, $p<.05$). This increase reinforces the growth of management flexibility for making subcontracting decisions.

Departmental Rules and Regulations

Most of the contracts studied contained statements about the establishment and modification of departmental rules and regulations. Rynecki and Morse indicated that 79 percent of their contracts concerned such provisions while the current study found 78 percent to have rules and regulations language. The earlier research showed that a little over one-third (36 percent) of the contracts contained language that gave the employer the exclusive right to create and modify rules and regulations for the department. The proportion of CBAs containing that provision had significantly increased by 1991. In the current study, 53 percent provided for rules and regulations to be the sole right of management ($z=3.466$, $p<.001$, Table 10).

Table 10
Departmental Rules and Regulations

Type Clause	1981	1991	% Change	Significance
Exclusive Mgt Right	36%	53%	+17	$z = 3.466$ $p<.001$
Notify of Change	27%	22%	–5	n.s.
Confer on Change	16%	2%	–14	$z = 4.384$ $p<.0001$
Negotiate Change	4%	1%	–3	n.s.
None	21%	22%	+1	n.s.

The issue of written policies and procedures, in general, blossomed in the late 1970s and early 1980s as a result of vicarious liability lawsuits against the police and the concomitant growth of law enforcement accreditation (Carter & Sapp, 1992b). Because police agencies began promulgating written directives with greater vigor, the issue became more visible and, consequently, appeared at many negotiating tables. According to interviews with Police Officer Association presidents during the course of the study, the promulgation of rules and regulations most appropriately rests with management. However, labor groups wanted the issue formally discussed to ensure that rules would not be established that infringed on employee rights.[7]

Earlier contracts were much more likely to place requirements on management before rules and regulations could be changed. Rynecki and Morse noted that 27 percent of their contracts contained provisions for management to notify the union of the implementation of new rules and regulations or changes in current ones. That requirement was also found in 22 percent of the 1991 agreements.

In 1981, 16 percent of the contracts called for management and labor to confer on any proposed changes or new rules and regulations. A significant decrease was noted in the 1991 contracts in which only two percent contained such provisions (z=4.384, p<.0001). A requirement for negotiation of any new rules and regulations and any changes to existing rules was found in four percent of the 1981 contracts and one percent of the 1991 agreements; however, that decrease was not statistically significant.

Seniority Clauses

Issues of seniority have always been volatile in labor negotiations. In the 1981 study, approximately 61 percent of the contracts contained clauses with provisions covering issues of seniority. Another 13 percent mentioned seniority without express language for its application. In the 1991 study, the percentage with provisions for seniority had decreased to slightly less than one-half (49.4 percent) of the agreements and 30 percent of the contracts mentioned seniority without corresponding application language. Overall the number of contracts containing no seniority language decreased from 26 percent to 21 percent (Table 11).

Table 11
Seniority

Type Clause	1981	1991	% Change	Significance
Exclusive Determinant	39%	10%	–29	z = 6.528 p<.0001
Factor in Primary Areas	36%	26%	–10	z = 2.124 p<.05
Determinant In Secondary	36%	36%	0	n.s.
One Factor in Secondary	24%	6%	–18	z = 4.687 p<.0001
No Seniority Language	26%	21%	–5	n.s.

The area of greatest change was in the inclusion of language that provided for seniority as the exclusive determinant in staff reductions, shift assignments, transfers, promotions, and other major personnel actions. In the earlier study, 39 percent of the contracts contained exclusive determinant language. In the current research, only ten percent had such language. This decrease is statistically significant at the .0001 level (z= 6.528, p<.0001).

Another decrease was noted in the use of seniority as a factor in primary personnel actions such as layoffs, recalls, promotions, shift assignments, and transfers. The decrease of 36 percent to 26 percent was statistically significant (z=2.124,

$p<.05$). There was no change in the percentage (36 percent) of the collective bargaining agreements that included seniority as the primary determinant in secondary issues such as leave, assignment of overtime, and vacation preferences.

The obvious question is why have these changes occurred. Seniority has long been an anchored provision in the labor movement, yet important statistically significant reductions of seniority clauses occurred as an exclusive primary determinant for various personnel actions. One reason has been hard negotiations by police management to eliminate the provisions. A second reason appears to be the trade-off of seniority issues for increases in benefits. Perhaps most profound, however, appears to be the professional growth of the police. That is, interviews and survey comments infer that police officers recognize that there are professional requirements and mandates of expertise that take precedence over seniority. Moreover, police officers appear to have a strong professional self-confidence and general feelings of occupational security that diminish the feeling that seniority is a necessity.[8] Finally, during the 1980s police departments generally experienced a growth in new officers as a result of both attrition and expansion. With an increased number of highly educated officers being hired and the average length of service decreasing (hence distinctions between levels of seniority being less pronounced), the newer cadre of officers simply did not appear to be as concerned with seniority as were their predecessors. The authors stress that the data in this study offer no empirical support for these observations. Rather, they are a product of integrated comments from the survey, site visits and interviews.

Sick Leave Requirements

Rynecki and Morse expressly examined sick leave as an example of a benefit clause that could be a source of conflict in negotiations and contract administration. Their study found 94 percent of the CBAs contained one or more clauses related to sick leave. The current study found that 91 percent of the agreements had sick leave clauses (or language)—a reduction that was not statistically significant. Closer examination analyzed three types of clause language related to the administration and management of sick leave.

The first clause was the requirement for notice of absence due to sickness. The common language for this requirement specified a period of time in which officers were required to report absence due to illness (for example, a provision may require that an officer may have to call in sick at least two hours before the beginning of his/her shift). In the earlier study, notice of absence requirements were evident in 48 percent of the contracts studied. In the current research, notice of absence requirements had increased to 61 percent ($z=2.596$ $p<.01$, Table 12) indicating the desire for greater planning and accountability by management.

Table 12
Sick Leave Requirements

Type Clause	1981	1991	% Change	Significance
Additional Reasons	48%	24%	–24	z = 4.962 p<.0001
Notice of Absence	48%	61%	+13	z = 2.596 p<.01
Documentation	30%	56%	+26	z = 5.480 p<.0001
Other Provisions	37%	11%	–26	z = 5.867 p<.0001
No Reference to Sick Leave	6%	9%	+3	n.s.

The second area, additional reasons for sick leave usage, examined the variety of reasons for which sick leave was allowed beyond the actual illness of an officer. Additional areas included pregnancy leave not otherwise covered under a maternity clause, family illness, funeral leave, and medical or dental appointments. The previous research noted that 48 percent of the contracts contained other reasons allowed for use of sick leave. By 1991, the proportion of collective bargaining agreements with specified additional reasons had decreased by one-half to 24 percent (z=4.962, p<.0001). This was surprising given the general trends of sick leave usage. One explanation may be the increased availability of personal days to deal with these other circumstances. Another likely explanation is that the collateral circumstances in which sick leave is permitted has become a matter of policy (by either the department or parent jurisdiction). In departments where it has become a matter of policy, the need for a contractual provision is virtually eliminated.

The third area, documentation of reasons or proof of absence, included limits on the duration of undocumented absences, the length of time required before documentation is mandatory, and the type of documentation required. The 1991 study indicated a significant increase in the requirement for documentation. The proportion of contracts with this requirement increased from 30 percent in 1981 to 56 percent in 1991 (z=5.480, p<.0001).

Observations during site visits, interviews, and anecdotal evidence appear to explain this increase for documentation. First, there has been a general increase in the number of sick days afforded to employees as a result of the bargaining process. As a concession for this increased expense, management wanted to ensure that those who took sick leave were, in fact, ill. A second factor is the rapidly increasing cost of health care benefits. It was felt by some executives that documentation of sick leave would serve as a means of accountability related to health care costs.

Over the period between the two studies, the focus apparently was on refining the language of the contracts and reducing the numbers of exceptions and unusual applications of sick leave. Clauses containing language referring to sick leave, but not in one of the administrative areas listed above, decreased from 37 percent in 1981 to only 11 percent in 1991 (z=5.867, p<.0001).

Cost of Living Adjustments

The inclusion of an automatic cost of living adjustment (COLA) clause in law enforcement union contracts appears to be a practice that is disappearing. In 1981, Rynecki and Morse found COLA clauses in only 19 percent of the contracts they studied. In the current project that percentage had dropped significantly to only five percent (z=3.969, p<.0001, Table 13).

Table 13
Cost of Living Adjustments

Type Clause	1981	1991	% Change	Significance
General COLA	3%	3%	0	n.s.
Restricted COLA	16%	2%	–14	z= 4.384 p<.0001
No Language	81%	95%	+14	z= 3.969 p<.0001

There was no change in the proportion of contracts containing provisions for a general COLA—three percent in both studies. However, when the contracts were analyzed for provisions related to a restricted COLA, the results were significantly different. The contracts with restrictions contained COLA provisions but placed restrictions on the adjustments not found in the general cost of living adjustment clauses. Restricted cost of living adjustment provisions included limits on the number of payments, the overall amount of any adjustment, and the duration of adjustment periods. The decrease in contracts with restrictions on COLA was from 16 percent in 1981 to two percent in 1991 (z=4.384, p<.0001).

The change in the restricted COLA appears to be offset by the increase in non-compensation benefits. Moreover, concerns about fiscal exigency also appear to have affected the presence of COLA clauses.

Police Education and Training

Education and training for police officers continues to be a topic of interest. The need for higher education and more specialized training is generally accepted in law enforcement (Carter & Sapp, 1991). Collective bargaining agreements also reflect this concern. In 1981, Rynecki and Morse found that 81 percent of the contracts they studied contained some type of provision directed toward police officer education and training. The current study found the same. However, there were some significant changes in the various provisions concerned with education and training.

As shown in Table 14, in the area of training, some of the contracts contain provisions for job training beyond that normally offered for recruits. This broad training provision was noted in 51 percent of the 1981 contracts but in only 25 percent of the current ones (z=5.356, p<.0001). The decrease in contract language requiring broad training most likely reflects the general acceptance of the need for training, the widespread training offered by most law enforcement agencies, and training requirements mandated in most states by POST (Police Officer Standards and Training) boards.

Table 14
Police Education and Training

Type Clause	1981	1991	% Change	Significance
Broad Training	51%	25%	–26	z = 5.356 p<.0001
Tuition Reimbursement	31%	41%	+10	z=2.101 p<.05
Education Incentive Pay	46%	42%	–4	n.s.
Leave of Absence	25%	13%	–12	z = 2.924 p<.01
No Language	19%	19%	0	n.s.

In the area of education, a shift was noted in tuition reimbursement and education incentive pay. The proportion of contracts including provisions for tuition reimbursement increased from 31 to 41 percent, between the studies (z=2.101, p<.05). At the same time the provisions for tuition reimbursement were increasing, the percentage of contracts providing for education incentive pay declined somewhat from 46 percent in the earlier study to 42 percent in the latest. This proportion is somewhat lower than that for the entire population of law enforcement agencies serving 50,000 or more (as opposed to those agencies in the survey population that had CBAs). In an earlier survey, Carter, Sapp and Stephens (1989) found that 54 percent of the agencies offered education incentive pay.

While not statistically significant, this difference probably reflects the increasing numbers of law enforcement agencies that require college education at some level before hiring or for promotion. The lack of statistical significance is most likely the result of a slow evolution of this trend (Carter, Sapp & Stephens, 1989). Another reflection of the increased educational requirements for employment or promotion is the drop in the proportion of contracts providing for educational leaves of absences. Educational leaves usually are limited to a period of not more than one year with full pay and allowances for the officer who is engaged in a full-time educational degree program. Most contracts also require the officer to return for full-time employment for a specified period following the leave. This period of obligated employment may range from a few months to several years. In 1981, 25 percent of the contracts had such a provision. By the 1991 study, 13 percent contained an educational leave of absence provision ($z=2.924$, $p<.01$). It appears from both the current study and previous research (Carter, Sapp & Stephens, 1989) that this difference has been largely influenced by policy change. As a result of the policy, there was no need for a contract provision. Another explanation is that with increased educational levels of new officers, the need for educational leave of absence was diminished. The result is most likely a function of both of these factors.

No-Strike Clauses

In the general area of no-strike clauses, very little change occurred in the time between the two studies. Changes that did take place were all favorable to management. Approximately 69 percent of the earlier contracts and 73 percent of the current ones contained language that specifically defined the meaning of strikes, although this change was not statistically significant. There were, however, significant differences in the proportion of collective bargaining agreements containing prohibitions on "sympathy strikes" (i.e., when a collective bargaining unit strikes in a show of support for another union's job actions). The 1981 study found such language in only one percent of the agreements while the current study identified sympathy strike bans in seven percent (3.657, $p<.001$). The differences in no-strike clauses are depicted in Table 15.

Table 15
No-Strike Clauses

Type Clause	1981	1991	% Change	Significance
Strike Defined	69%	73%	+4	n.s.
Sympathy Strikes	1%	7%	+6	$z = 3.657$ $p<.001$
Discipline of Strikers	32%	38%	+6	n.s.
Union Action Required	20%	30%	+10	$z = 2.368$ $p<.01$
Union Responsible	6%	5%	–1	n.s.
Union Liability Limited	11%	1%	–10	$z = 3.703$ $p<.0001$
Other Language	8%	5%	–3	n.s.
No Language	21%	26%	+5	n.s.

There was a significant increase in the number of CBAs that required the union to take positive and affirmative action to end any strike. The increase was from 20 percent to 30 percent between the studies ($z=2.368$, $p<.01$). There was also a significant decrease in language that limited the union's liability for failing to take affirmative action to end a strike. Eleven percent of earlier contracts had liability limits while such limits were found in only one percent of the newer contracts ($z=3.703$, $p<.0001$).

Several provisions related to the issue of strikes and prohibitions against strikes were similar in the two studies. The proportion of agreements with statements that employees who strike may be disciplined was 32 percent in 1981 and 38 percent in 1991. Contracts that contained provisions indicating that the union might be legally responsible for damages or fines and penalties when a strike took place remained virtually unchanged. In 1991, 26 percent of the contracts made no reference to strikes while in the previous study 21 percent did not contain strike language. Eight percent of the earlier contracts contained other language and provisions concerning strikes while five percent had such language in the recent research. None of these differences were, however, statistically significant.

Evidence gathered throughout the course of the research project suggests that an important reason for more direct language dealing with strikes is not based on public safety concerns, but on passage of state laws (and sometimes local ordinances) prohibiting strikes. The presence of the contractual provision appears to be a reinforcing factor.

Conclusions

The clauses and provisions of police collective bargaining agreements analyzed in the current research provide a number of indications of likely future developments in this critical area. The changes were diverse and do not permit one to inextricably conclude that either management or labor prevailed. Almost every difference favorable to management noted between the 1981 and 1991 studies is counterbalanced by a movement that favors the labor side of the equation. Because negotiation is a process of give-and-take, the degree of counterbalancing in these findings should not be surprising. Perhaps the best assessment is that police management-labor differences have moved closer to a homeostatic relationship) over the past decade.

Management rights clauses have moved toward more comprehensive statements of such rights and away from provisions that make management decisions and actions subject to grievance and arbitration processes. The move toward less restrictive definitions of grievances, which in turn provides more variance for employee grievances and appeals has, however, contributed to that movement. Clearly, there are fewer contracts with maintenance of standards and benefits language, a change that would favor management. A counterbalance to fewer statements of maintenance of benefits and standards is the increase in contract provisions for disciplinary procedures and appeals to be subject to contract provisions.

In the areas of layoffs and recalls, labor clearly benefits from the movement toward use of seniority for these difficult decisions. Management gains, on the other hand, from the decrease in the use of seniority in other critical personnel decisions. Management gains from sick leave provisions that require notice and documentation while labor benefits from expanded uses of sick leave beyond the area of officer illness.

Some of the clauses analyzed are likely to disappear from future bargaining agreements as increased policy decisions are formalized and legislation is passed. Only five percent of the contracts analyzed in this study contained cost of living adjustment clauses. Those are likely to be dropped in the future due to the interactive effects of budget constraints on one hand and the increased use of merit raises on the other hand. Similarly, contract provisions concerning subcontracting are also likely to diminish. Management's right to subcontract is clearly established and further substantive negotiations are unlikely in this area.

Additional clauses provide benefits to both sides with a single provision. In the area of police training and education, the language seen in the current contracts provides for tuition reimbursement at an increased rate while the use of education incentive pay decreased slightly. These changes are probably best viewed as benefiting both sides about equally.

Strike provisions and union liability and action requirements are likely to continue to be a source of management pressure in negotiations. Management rights clauses dealing with the right of management to establish and change rules and regulations also are likely to continue in favor of management. Staffing clauses also increasingly contain language recognizing management's rights to staff units and departments as management chooses. Some clear changes have occurred in CBA provisions. While they appear to be foundations for predictive trends, they are still subject to intervening variables that could change their course. Despite this caveat, one may conclude that the police collective bargaining process is stabilizing. Management's seat at the collective bargaining table is increasingly one of true negotiation rather than reaction.

Notes

This study was conducted for the Police Executive Research Forum with funding support from the Ford Foundation. The opinions expressed in this paper are those of the authors and do not necessarily reflect those of the Police Executive Research Forum membership or staff or those of the Ford Foundation. The authors express their appreciation to Darrel Stephens, Executive Director of PERF, for his leadership and continued support of applied research in policing.

[1] While in many states public safety organizations cannot form unions, they can form employee associations that may collectively bargain on such things as salary, benefits and working conditions as well as enter into formal agreements with the employer. The implication is that employee associations are not permitted to take job actions—such as strikes or work slowdowns—that unions are. In reality, the distinctions are minimal for descriptive purposes. Thus, for purposes of readability, the term *union* will be used synonymously in this paper with employee associations and collective bargaining units. Similarly, in many states, public sector employee groups may not enter into a contract; rather, they enter into collective bargaining agreements or agree to a memorandum of understanding. Once again, in this paper, *contract* will be used synonymously with these terms for purposes of readability.

[2] For a good discussion of the police labor movement and the processes of labor negotiations, see Gaines, Southerland and Angell, 1991:301-304.

[3] A brief explanation of the returned contracts is warranted. There were 323 agencies in the responding population that indicated they had a CBA. Of these, 301 (93%) submitted a copy of the CBA for content analysis. In some cases, agencies had multiple contracts with sworn officer groups. For example, a department may have one CBA with the Police Officers' Association and a second agreement with a Sergeants' and Lieutenants' Association or some other group of sworn personnel. As in the case of the Rynecki and Morse (1981) study, all CBAs with sworn groups were analyzed in order to enhance the reliability of the comparisons.

[4] The data and methods of both studies meet the assumptions for the Z-test of Differences Between Proportions. The data tables report the results in percentages rather than proportions simply to enhance the readability of the tables. In some tables the total percentages are either less than or more than 100%. The primary reason for this disparity is that some contracts did not contain the specific provisions analyzed in this paper for comparison to Rynecki and Morse. Conversely, some contracts had multiple provisions—a factor also experienced in the Rynecki and Morse (1981) analysis. Some minor differences are also the result of rounding.

[5] The specific benefits and standards that these general clauses can include encompasses a wide range, such as COLA, vacation, insurance, seniority, and so forth. The point to note is that a Maintenance of Standards and Benefits clause is a general provision affecting conditions prior to the CBA containing the clause.

[6] At the time of this writing there is a bill pending before the U.S. Congress mandating that all states enact a Police Officers' Bill of Rights. Should the federal legislation pass, it mandates that the states that do not enact a Police Officers' Bill of Rights will have the federal provisions apply. While there are several different specifications in the various Bills of Rights, the following is a summary example of the typical provisions: (1) Interrogations of officers accused of rule violations shall be done in a timely manner; (2) Accused officers must be informed of investigating officers and the officer in charge of the internal investigation; (3) An officer must be informed of the nature of the investigation before an interrogation begins; (4) The length of interrogations must be reasonable and include rest breaks; (5) Officers cannot be threatened with transfer, dismissal or other disciplinary action as a means of obtaining information during the interrogation; (6) Officers may have counsel or a representative of the employee organization present during the interrogation; (7) The interrogation must be recorded with no "off-the-record" questions; (8) Officers accused of criminal offenses must be advised of the *Miranda* rights; (9) Officers being investigated may receive an exact copy of any written statement he/she signed or a copy of the interrogation recording; (10) An officer cannot be ordered to submit to a polygraph examination.

[7] As the Secretary/Treasurer of one national police labor organization stated during a presentation to police executives with respect to drug testing policy and procedures, "It's okay to get one of our guys, but you've got to get him *right*" (emphasis in original).

[8] The authors feel—but certainly cannot prove—that one important element of this is the increased educational levels of police officers (see Carter, Sapp & Stephens, 1989).

[9] Ironically, documentation of sick leave could actually increase health care costs because it would require a visit to the physician to obtain the documentation in cases in which medical services might not otherwise be needed.

References

Ayres, M. and R. Ayres (1981). "Police on Strike: What Triggers Their Walkouts?" *FBI Law Enforcement Bulletin*, 50(1).

Bartel, A. and D. Lewin (1980). "Wages and Unionism in the Public Sector: The Case of the Police." *The Review of Economics and Statistics*, (March):53-59.

Bell, D. (1981). "Police Collective Bargaining: Perspective for the 1980s." *Journal of Police Science and Administration*, 9(3):296-305.

Bloom, D. (1981). "Collective Bargaining, Compulsory Arbitration, and Salary Settlements in the Public Sector: The Case of New Jersey's Municipal Police Officers." *Journal of Labor Research*, 2(2):369-84.

Burpo, J. (1981). "The Police Labor Movement." *FBI Law Enforcement Bulletin*, 50(1):9-12.

Butler, R. and R. Ehrenberg (1981). "Estimating the Narcotic Effect of Public Impasse Procedures." *Industrial and Labor Relations Review*, 35(1):3-20.

Carter, D. and A. Sapp (1992a). "The Current Status of Police Collective Bargaining: A National Management Survey," in W. Tafoya (ed.), *The Future of Policing*. Washington, DC: U.S. Government Printing Office.

Carter, D. and A. Sapp (1992b). "Police Chief Perspectives of Law Enforcement Accreditation: Findings of a National Study." A paper presented at the annual meeting of the Academy of Criminal Justice Sciences.

Carter, D. and A. Sapp (1990). "The Evolution of Higher Education in Law Enforcement: Preliminary Findings from a National Study." *Journal of Criminal Justice Education*, 1(1):59-86.

Carter, D., A. Sapp and D. Stephens (1989). *The State of Police Education: Policy Directions for the 21st Century*. Washington, DC: Police Executive Research Forum.

Connolly, M. (1986). "The Impact of Final-Offer Arbitration on Wage Outcomes of Public Safety Personnel." *Journal of Collective Negotiations*, 15(3):253-62.

Delaney, J. and P. Feuille (1984). "Police Interest Arbitration: Awards and Issues." *The Arbitration Journal*, 39(2):14-24.

Feuille, P. and J. Delaney (1986). "Collective Bargaining, Interest Arbitration, and Police Salaries." *Industrial and Labor Relations Review*, 39(2):228-40.

Feuille, P., J. Delaney and W. Hendricks (1985). "Police Bargaining, Arbitration, and Fringe Benefits." *Journal of Labor Research*, 6(1):1-20.

Gaines, L., M. Southerland and J. Angell (1991). *Police Administration*. New York, NY: McGraw Hill.

Gallagher, D. and P. Veglahn (1987). "The Effect of Collective Bargaining on Wage Dispersion Between Municipal Police Departments." *Journal of Collective Negotiations*, 16(4):327-41.

Juris, H. and P. Feuille (1973). *The Impact of Police Unions*. Washington, DC: National Institute of Law Enforcement and Criminal Justice.

Kruger, D. and H. Jones (1981). "Compulsory Interest Arbitration in the Public Sector: An Overview." *Journal of Collective Negotiation*, 10(4):355-80.

Leonard, W. (1976). *Basic Social Statistics*. St. Paul, MN: West Publishing Company.

Rvnecki, S. and M. Morse (1981). *Police Collective Bargaining Agreements: A National Management Survey* (Revised and Expanded Edition). Washington, DC: National League of Cities and Police Executive Research Forum.

Rynecki, S., D. Cairns and D. Cairns (1978). *Police Collective Bargaining Agreements: A National Management Survey*. Washington, DC: National League of Cities and Police Executive Research Forum.

Sapp, A. (1980). *An Exploratory and Descriptive Analysis of Grievance Procedures in Law Enforcement Collective Bargaining* (Unpublished Doctoral dissertation). Huntsville, TX: Sam Houston State University.

Sapp, A., D. Carter and D. Stephens (1990). *Law Enforcement Collective Bargaining Agreements: Preliminary Findings from a National Survey*. Washington, DC: Police Executive Research Forum.

Wolkinson, B., K. Chelst and L. Shepard (1985). "Arbitration Issues in the Consolidation of Police and Fire Bargaining Units." *The Arbitration Journal*, 40(4):43-54.

The Effectiveness of Civilian Review: Observations on Recent Trends and New Issues Regarding the Civilian Review of the Police

Samuel Walker
University of Nebraska at Omaha

Vic W. Bumphus
Michigan State University

Civilian review of the police has been a controversial issue in policing for nearly forty years (Terrill, 1991). The concept is defined as a procedure under which citizen complaints against police officers are reviewed at some point by persons who are not sworn officers. Virtually all proposals for civilian review were defeated in the 1960s, but in the last few years the concept has spread rapidly among big-city police departments. By 1992 over two-thirds (68%) of the police departments in the 50 largest cities had some form of civilian review (Walker & Bumphus, 1991; Walker, 1992). This paper reports the findings of a survey of the 50 largest cities and discusses the important new questions raised by this data.

The central issue regarding civilian review has traditionally been the question of whether it is appropriate for citizens to be involved in the complaint process. The police have opposed civilian review on the grounds that the concept intrudes on their professional autonomy, that persons who are not police officers are not competent to evaluate police actions, and out of fear of greater scrutiny of police behavior. The civilian review issue has also been a civil rights issue, pitting the African-American community against predominantly white police departments.

To a great extent, these traditional issues have been settled. The city councils in two-thirds of the largest cities have, in effect, made a legislative finding that some form of civilian review is an appropriate response to the problem of police misconduct. This development shifts the ground to a different set of questions. The central question concerns the effectiveness of civilian review. Does it work? Or, more precisely, is one form of complaint review more effective than others? This raises a host of subsidiary questions. How is effectiveness defined? What measures of effectiveness are appropriate? How useful is official data on citizen complaints and the disposition of complaints? This paper examines these and other new questions raised by the recent developments in the area of civilian review.

The 50-City Survey: Findings

Methodology

In the spring of 1991 a survey was conducted of citizen complaint procedures in the 50 largest cities in the United States (Walker & Bumphus, 1991). An initial telephone inquiry determined whether the police department had any form of citizen input in the complaint process. If the answer was yes, the respondent was asked to describe the process and also to forward official documents describing the complaint process. On the basis of the telephone interviews and the official documents, citizen complaint procedures were then analyzed and categorized according to a three-part classification system.[1]

Principal Findings

The survey found some form of civilian review in 30 of the 50 police departments. Between April 1991 and October 1992, civilian review procedures were adopted in four additional cities, bringing the total to 34, or 68 percent of the total (Walker, 1992).[2] The survey also found an accelerating trend toward civilian review. Nineteen of the 34 (55.8%) have been established since 1986, with eight established between 1990 and 1992 alone. An earlier survey (West, 1988) identified a total of 15 civilian review, or external review procedures in the entire country by 1987.

There is some ambiguity regarding the exact date that some civilian review procedures were created. In some instances, city councils passed an ordinance creating a new procedure in one year but did not actually begin its operation until the following year. In some cities (New York City [Kahn, 1975], Chicago, Milwaukee) preexisting units or agencies were revised several times over the years. The survey defined the effective creation date as the point when non-sworn persons gained some involvement in the complaint process.[3]

Civilian review appears to be a nationwide phenomenon, with no geographic region underrepresented. The demographic characteristics of cities also do not appear to be a factor. Civilian review procedures exist in cities with small African-American populations (Indianapolis, Minneapolis) as well as those with large minority populations (Detroit, Atlanta). The trend toward civilian review also appears to be an international phenomenon, at least in English-speaking countries, with the establishment of new procedures in England, Canada and Australia in the 1980s. The United Kingdom created a national system, the Police Complaints Authority (PCA) in 1985 (Goldsmith, 1991).

Types of Civilian Review Procedures

The survey also found considerable variation among civilian review procedures in terms of the degree of civilian input and operating procedures. The degree of civilian input is the crucial factor in civilian review. "Degree" in this context refers to the exact point in the complaint process at which non-sworn persons participate. The three key points are: (1) the initial fact-finding investigation; (2) the review of investigative reports and the power to recommend action by the chief executive; (3) the review of decisions already taken by the chief executive. The survey developed a three-part classification system (Walker & Bumphus, 1991). This closely resembled classification systems developed by Kerstetter (1985) and Patterson (1991).[4]

Class I systems are those in which the initial fact-finding investigation is done by individuals who are not sworn police officers. Their reports go to a person (or persons) who is also not a sworn officer, and who makes a recommendation to the chief executive for action. Class II systems are those in which the fact-finding investigation is done by sworn officers, but the recommendation to the chief executive is made by a person (or persons) who is not a sworn officer. Class III systems are those in which the initial fact-finding and recommendation are done by sworn officers; if the complaining party is unsatisfied with the disposition of the complaint, he or she may appeal that decision to a person who is not a sworn officer, or group of persons that includes at least some non-sworn persons.

Since the 1991 survey was conducted, two cities (Seattle and San Jose) have created "auditor" systems that do not fit neatly into any of the three classes. Under these systems, a non-sworn person has the authority to oversee the complaint process, and may make recommendations to police investigators, but has no power to make recommendations for discipline. The auditor approach fits the classification system created by Patterson (1991:276).

General Features

Several features are common to all existing civilian review procedures. First, none have the power to impose discipline on a police officer and can only make recommendations to the police chief executive (Patterson, 1991).[5] Granting a civilian review agency the power to impose discipline would require a change in existing civil service laws, as well as collective bargaining contracts in most cities.

Second, 26 of the 30 procedures identified in 1991 were established by municipal ordinance or state statute. This represents a significant change from the pattern in the 1950s and 1960s in which the first two important procedures, in Philadelphia (Coxe, 1965; Hudson, 1972; Terrill, 1988; Walker, 1990) and New York City (Kahn, 1975), were created by executive order. Because they did not represent a decision by a majority of the elected representatives, they were politically and administratively vulnerable. The Philadelphia Police Advisory Board (PAB) was abolished by the executive order of a subsequent mayor. An expanded and more civilian version of the New York City CCRB was abolished by referendum. Thus, current civilian review procedures are on more solid legal footing and represent a broader community consensus than earlier procedures.

The extent of this community consensus is indicated by a 1992 public opinion poll that found broad public support for civilian review. The Louis Harris (1992) organization surveyed 1,248 adults and found that 80 percent favored review of citizen complaints by mixed teams of police and non-sworn investigators; 15 percent supported investigations by non-sworn persons only, while only four percent supported the traditional approach of having citizen complaints reviewed entirely by police officers. Third, the survey revealed some of the problems involved in the commonly used terminology. The public and the media generally refer to these groups as "civilian review boards."

The national survey of civilian review procedures also found that the term civilian review board is a misnomer. Not all of the existing review procedures involve a multi-member *board*. Several are municipal agencies with a single director (Walker & Bumphus, 1991). The generic term "civilian review *procedure*" is a more accurate descriptor than civilian review board.

The term "independent" is also extremely ambiguous and the source of much misunderstanding. The Cincinnati Office of Municipal Investigations is independent in the sense that it is an agency separate from the police department. The Professional Standards Section of the Detroit Police Department, on the other hand, is under the jurisdiction of the Board of Police Commissioners and, thus, might be viewed by some observers as not independent (Littlejohn, 1981). However, the investigative fact-finding in Detroit is done by persons who are not sworn officers. Consequently, the 50-city survey deemed it independent. The Kansas City Office of Citizen Complaints (1983) is a separate municipal agency, with a director who is not a sworn officer and an office in a building separate from police headquarters. However, the fact-finding in Kansas City is done by sworn officers in the internal affairs unit. This makes the review of complaints in Kansas City much less independent of the police department than the procedure in Detroit.

Unanswered Questions

Explaining the Patterns of Growth

The recent growth of civilian review procedures has not received close attention by police scholars. With the exception of Terrill (1991) and West (1988), there is no general overview of this rapidly changing area of policing. There is a detailed analysis of the creation of only one of the current systems (Littlejohn, 1981). Occasional surveys of various agencies are conducted by private organizations (New York Civil Liberties Union, 1993) but the resulting reports often lack important data and do not reach a wide audience.

The agenda for future research on civilian review includes, at minimum, explaining the recent growth of the phenomenon and developing more detailed comparative data.[6]

Some observations about the history of civilian review suggest the direction that research might take. In the 1960s, the two major civilian review procedures were abolished. Both had been created by liberal Republican mayors in response to the demands by civil rights forces and both were abolished primarily as a result of pressure from local police unions (Hudson, 1972; Terrill, 1988). In the case of New York City, a union-sponsored referendum abolished the civilian-dominated CCRB, leaving in place a board not dominated by civilians (Kahn, 1975). Because of the success of the police unions, many observers concluded that civilian review was essentially dead as a possible reform measure. A change evidently occurred in 1974, with the creation of two important review procedures (Detroit, Chicago). They were followed by twelve others over the next decade.[7] Since 1986, the spread of civilian review has been very rapid. The momentum of this trend appears to be accelerating, with the 1991 Rodney King beating by Los Angeles police officers and its aftermath providing an additional boost. No systematic data exists on cities smaller than the fifty largest. Impressionistic evidence suggests that there is increasing interest in civilian review in medium-sized cities.[8]

The trend of events suggests a significant change in the balance of power in the context of municipal politics. The most obvious possible explanation would be the growth of African-American political power, particularly in those cities where blacks constitute a majority of voters and where black mayors have been elected. Black political leadership was undoubtedly a factor in the creation of civilian review procedure in Detroit (Littlejohn, 1981) and Atlanta. Yet this cannot account for the creation of civilian review in cities with relatively small black communities (Indianapolis, Minneapolis, Seattle) and the absence civilian review in some cities with relatively large black communities (Philadelphia). Nor is the election of a black mayor the critical variable, in and of itself. Philadelphia and Los Angeles have both elected black mayors but remain without civilian review procedures.

Many observers argue that the creation of a civilian review procedure requires a well-organized political effort by a coalition of community groups. This was the case in Indianapolis (Gradison, 1989) and Minneapolis, but it fails to account for the absence of civilian review cities with similar community coalitions, such as Los Angeles (Ripston, 1991) and Philadelphia (Coxe, 1988). A well-organized coalition has had great difficulty in strengthening the existing system in New York City (Siegel, 1991). In short, a well-organized demand for civilian review is probably a necessary condition, but not itself a sufficient one.

One major factor has been the apparent decline in the power of police unions, at least on this issue. Police unions were the principal force in defeating civilian review proposals in New York City (Kahn, 1975) and Philadelphia (Terrill, 1988) in the 1960s. Yet they have been increasingly unsuccessful in most cities. In fact, with the two most recently created review procedures, Seattle (Taylor, 1991) and Denver (Law Enforcement News, 1992), the police union either actively supported the proposal or chose not to oppose it. In both cases, the police union concluded that some form of civilian review would be adopted in any event and that it could live with the present proposal.

Generally speaking, police chiefs do not appear to be active opponents of civilian review. This represents a significant change from the 1960s when the International Association of Chiefs of Police adopted an official statement opposing civilian review (Police Chief, 1964). The attitude of the big-city chiefs is best indicated by the official position of the Police Executive Research Forum (1981), which has urged police departments to establish and maintain effective systems of discipline. Although it has not endorsed civilian review, PERF has not officially opposed the concept either.

A case-study approach could serve to illuminate the process by which civilian review procedures are established. In virtually every city, creation of a procedure is the result of some immediate controversy (usually a shooting or physical force incident). In each case, however, there had been a number of similar incidents in the past, each usually followed by a proposal for civilian review (Gradison, 1989; Taylor, 1991). The relevant question, then, becomes what changes led to the creation of a civilian review procedure? A case-study approach could identify whether the most important change or changes involved: (1) new mayoral leadership; (2) a new composition on city council; (3) a new police chief; (4) changes in the strategy and tactics of civilian review advocates; (5) some other relevant factor.

The Effectiveness of Civilian Review

The most frequently asked question about civilian review is whether it works. At present, it is impossible to provide a definitive answer to that question. There are no thorough, independent evaluations of the effectiveness of any procedure, much less any comparative studies. Studies by Hudson (1972) and Perez (1978; 1992) are limited by serious conceptual and methodological problems. An evaluation of the New York City CCRB by the Vera Institute (1989a, 1989b, 1988) addressed a limited range of issues.

The question of effectiveness raises a number of problems. First, there is no single entity known as "civilian review." As the 50-city survey found, there are three general categories and a number of variations within each category (Walker & Bumphus, 1991). Any attempt to measure effectiveness needs to take into account the possibility that one form of civilian review may prove to be more effective than other forms. Common sense suggests that procedures with greater resources, (e.g., number of staff) and powers (e.g., subpoena power) are more likely to be effective than other systems. By the same token, it would be dangerous to compare procedures solely on the basis of their formal structure and powers. One procedure that appears to be more ("independent" on paper may be undermined through administrative resistance and thus be less effective than another system that is nominally less "independent."

Second, defining effectiveness is problematic. There are several possible measures of effectiveness that are related to the different objectives of the concept. Maguire (1991:186) identifies four distinct objectives of civilian review. They include: (1) maintaining effective discipline of the police; (2) providing satisfactory resolution of individual complaints; (3) maintaining public confidence in the police; and (4) influencing police management by providing "feedback from consumers." A comprehensive evaluation of effectiveness would take into account all four of these dimensions of civilian review.

In the minds of its advocates, the primary objective of civilian review is to provide a more independent review of citizen complaints (1966). The assumption has been that persons who are not sworn police officers are likely to conduct a more thorough investigation of a complaint than a fellow officer. The so-called "blue curtain and the tendency of officers to cover up the misconduct of fellow officers has long been recognized as a phenomenon of the police officer subculture (Westley, 1970; New York Civil Liberties Union, 1990) and a barrier to effective discipline. Advocates of civilian review have assumed that the review of complaints by non-sworn officers will result in more disciplinary actions and an improvement in on-the-street police behavior (ACLU, 1966).

The Ambiguity of Official Data

One of the major problems confronting any attempt to evaluate the police complaint process (whether internal or external) is the ambiguous nature of official data on the number of complaints, the complaint rate (complaints per population or complaints per officer), the rate at which complaints are sustained, and the ultimate disciplinary actions taken, if any.

The number of complaints may reflect administrative procedures rather than police performance. In the wake of the Rodney King beating by Los Angles police officers in March, 1991, some observers noted that San Francisco had more citizen complaints than did the much larger Los Angeles police department (*New York Times*, 1991). It is entirely possible that the existence of a strong civilian review procedure in San Francisco brings forth more citizen complaints. In fact, a study by the ACLU in Los Angeles in 1992 found that the police department was actively discouraging citizen complaints (ACLU-Southern California, 1992). In New York City, the number of complaints increased tenfold between the mid-1960s and the mid-1970s. This enormous increase appears to be associated with administrative changes that made the complaint process more open and more accessible to the public (Kahn, 1975).

Two comments on this phenomenon are in order. First, a higher rate of complaints could be viewed as an indicator of success: it reflects that fact that citizens are more confident that they will receive a fair hearing and therefore file their complaints (ACLU, 1992; Crew, 1991). The New York Civil Liberties Union (1990:29-33) attributed the 50 percent decline in the number of complaints filed with the CCRB between 1985 and 1989 to declining public confidence in the CCRB itself. Second, police departments face the unpleasant fact that the better they do the worse they will look. A more open and responsive complaint system will probably generate more complaints.

The impact of administrative changes on the number of complaints is extremely complex. In Detroit the creation of a more independent review procedure produced an immediate increase in complaints, followed by a reduction (Littlejohn, 1981). A similar pattern was reported in Kansas City (Kansas City, Office of Citizen Complaints, 1983) and New York City (Kahn, 1975; New York Civil Liberties Union, 1990). The initial increase in complaints could be the result of greater public confidence in the effectiveness of the complaint process. The subsequent decline could be the result of either citizen disillusionment with the process or a genuine improvement in police conduct, with the civilian review procedure functioning as a genuine deterrent to misconduct. The interplay of complaint procedures and the volume and rate of complaints is, in short, highly complex and complicates any attempt at evaluation.

The official data on the number and rate of complaints is problematic because we do not have any baseline data on the actual number of incidents of police misconduct. This issue is a highly political question, with some people arguing that misconduct is pervasive, while others argue that it is a relatively infrequent event. The available research on this question is suggestive at best. Albert Reiss (1968; 1971) found that police officers used "undue force" relatively rarely: in only 37 of 3,,826 observed police encounters. This represented a rate of 5.9 for every 1,000 white citizens and 2.8 for every 1,000 black citizens. The New York City Civilian Complaint Review Board (1990:45-51) reported citizen complaints at rates ranging from a high of five per 10,000 to a low of one per 10,000 documented encounters between officers and citizens, depending on the neighborhood. These data suggest that excessive force is a statistically rare event. Reiss (1971:151), however, pointed out that instances of police abuse accumulate over time, creating the perception of police harassment. Official data on complaints has consistently indicated that racial minority males are disproportionately represented among complainants (New York Civilian Complaint Review Board, 1990). Thus, the perception of a pattern of police harassment is a major factor in conflict between the police and racial minority communities.

The Police Services Study (PSS), which included a more representative sample of police agencies, used a victimization survey and found that 13.6 percent of all respondents felt that they had been the victim of police mistreatment in the previous year (Whitaker, 1982). In certain respects this might appear to reflect a very high rate of police misconduct. A study of 911 calls in Minneapolis, for example, found that only 40 percent of the addresses in the city had any contact with the police (Sherman, 1987). Assuming for the moment that 13 percent of the population experienced some mistreatment, then a disturbingly high percentage of those with any contact at all would be the victim of misconduct. These observations are entirely speculative; it is dangerous to make estimates by combining the results of two unrelated surveys. Nonetheless, these observations are designed to highlight the absence of any systematic victimization data regarding police misconduct.

Only 30 percent of the PSS respondents who claimed to have been mistreated by the police filed a formal complaint about the incident (Whitaker, 1982). This figure bears a striking similarity to the 37 percent rate of reporting crimes to the police. Moreover, the reasons given for not filing complaints are very similar to the reasons for not reporting crimes (e.g., "wouldn't do any good," which was given by 43 percent of the respondents) (Whitaker, 1982; U.S. Department of Justice, 1991). Extrapolating these estimates to New York City (1990), one might estimate that even in the high complaint rate precincts there is some misconduct in 15 out of every 10,000 encounters. It is reasonable to conclude that official complaints received by police departments represent about one-third of all incidents of alleged police misconduct. An important research question involves whether the complaining/reporting rate is higher in some cities than others and whether the differences are associated with differences in the complaint process.

Even the raw number of citizen complaints is problematic. It is a truism that official police data on crime often reflect administrative practices rather than the actual behavior it purports to measure. An unknown number of crimes reported by citizens are unfounded by police. The recording of arrests also varies widely by department (Sherman & Glick, 1984). With respect to citizen complaints, a number of problems arise. First, there is evidence that some departments actively discourage the filing of complaints (ACLU-Southern California, 1992; Kahn, 1975). Second, commonly used terms are not standard across all departments. The San Francisco Office of Citizen Complaints (1991) distinguishes between "complaints" and "allegations." One complaint may involve several different allegations against one or more officers. In 1990, the New York City Civilian Complaint Review Board (1990:9) received 3,377 complaints involving 5,554 separate allegations. Clearly, then, comparisons in the absence of standardized definitions are problematic. Imagine an event in which three officers verbally and physically abuse one citizen. One department might record this as "one" incident or complaint, while another might record it as "six" complaints.

Police departments report very different rates at which citizen complaints are sustained. A citizen complaint may result in one of several outcomes. It is "substantiated" or "sustained" if the department agrees with all or some of the citizen's complaint. The officer is "exonerated" if the department agrees with the officer's version of the incident. The complaint is "not sustained" or "unfounded" if the investigation is unable to resolve the matter in the favor of either. Finally, many complaints are "dismissed" or "dropped," frequently because the complaining party fails to pursue the complaint or cooperate further with the investigation (New York, CCRB, 1990; San Diego, 1990).

The fact that a department sustains a relatively higher rate complaints may be a result of the fact that it receives relatively few complaints. The smaller number of complaints would presumably include a relatively higher proportion of more serious instances of misconduct that are presumptively more likely to be sustained. By the same token, a relatively low rate of sustaining complaints in a department may be a product of receiving a high volume of complaints that presumably includes a relatively lower percentage of more serious instances of misconduct.[9]

Any attempt to evaluate the effectiveness of a complaint review process needs to be incident-specific and seriousness-specific. Aggregate data on complaints and dispositions fail to take into account relevant distinctions between incidents. Common sense suggests that the unjustified use of physical force is far more serious than mere discourtesy. The use of racial or ethnic slurs is more serious than a neutral expression of discourtesy. A number of existing civilian review procedures, do divide complaints into two categories, according to seriousness (San Diego, 1990; Kansas City, 1983).

An important but hidden aspect of the complaint disposition process involves the lack of subsequent cooperation by the complaining party. In New York City, 35.4 percent of the complaints (1,197 out 3,377) were dropped because the complaint was formally withdrawn or the complainant was unavailable or uncooperative (New York City, 1990:16). Critics of the CCRB characterized these data as "alarming" (New York Civil Liberties Union, 1990:28). The high rate of non-cooperation is not entirely surprising. Failure of the victim to cooperate is one of the major reasons why criminal cases are dismissed. With respect to complaints about the police, however, the reasons for withdrawal or non-cooperation may reflect the behavior of the investigators. Complaint processing officials may discourage citizens through indifference, rudeness, or failure to act on complaints in a timely fashion. A telephone survey conducted by the Southern California ACLU (1992) found that Los Angeles Police Department officials actively subverted the complaint process, rarely providing the caller with the department's official toll-free telephone number for complaints. Even when cases are investigated, investigators from the police department's internal affairs unit or the civilian complaint agency make only a half-hearted attempt to locate the complaining party or potential witnesses.

In any event, an officially recorded disposition of "complainant unavailable" cannot be taken at face value. Advocates of civilian review argue that non-sworn investigators are likely to be more aggressive in following up on complaints and less hostile to complainants. While there are abundant *a priori* reasons for assuming this to be true (particularly the literature on the "blue curtain," [Westley, 1970]), there is at present no empirical evidence to support it.

This discussion highlights the point that the key element in the effectiveness of any complaint review system, whether internal or external, is the vigor of the investigative process. Presumably, this could be measured in terms of the number of witnesses contacted, the timeliness of the investigation, or other possible factors. At present, however, such data is not readily available. The formal administrative structure of any procedure (internal vs. external, independent vs. not independent, etc.) does not necessarily determine the vigor or the quality of investigations.

A study of the bias crimes unit of the New York City Police Department, however, does suggest that there is some relationship between the level of organizational commitment, the vigor of investigations, and case outcomes (Garofalo, 1991). The existence of a bias crimes unit reflected an organizational commitment to investigating hate-motivated crimes. Over 90 percent of the incidents investigated by the unit resulted in three or more follow-up investigative reports. Meanwhile, 76 percent of a comparable sample of non-bias crimes produced no investigative reports; only seven percent received three or more. The arrest rate for bias crimes was two and one-half to three times that of the non-bias crimes sample. In short, a greater formal organizational commitment produced more actual work that resulted in a measurable difference in outcomes.

Public Opinion About the Police

Because one of the purposes of civilian review is to enhance public confidence in the police, surveys of public opinion offer a potential evaluation technique. The simplest approach would be to compare citizens' attitudes toward their local police department in cities with different complaint procedures (e.g., cities with civilian review vs. those without). Previous surveys of public opinion indicated some city-by-city variations in citizen evaluations of local police departments (U.S. Department of Justice, 1977). Significantly, white and black attitudes tend to move in the same direction, suggesting that persons of different races evaluate their local police department on the basis of roughly the same criteria. It would be possible to correlate such differences with complaint procedures. In some instances, it might be possible to identify changes in public opinion about a local police department that is associated with the creation of, or the revision of, a civilian review procedure.

Police complaint procedures could also be evaluated through surveys of public knowledge about the complaint process (e.g., the existence of a complaint procedure; where complaints could be filed). One could reasonably hypothesize that a relatively higher level of public awareness reflects a more effective job of facilitating complaints on the part of the police department. A low level of citizen knowledge about the complaint procedure might suggest that the police department is actively discouraging the filing of complaints.

Another possible measure of effectiveness would be the satisfaction of citizens who have filed complaints. Douglas Perez (1978; 1992) adopted this approach, surveying citizens who had filed formal complaints, comparing the responses in cites with civilian review and cities without it.[10] His data indicated a higher level of satisfaction in the complaint process in those cities with civilian input, including citizens whose complaints were not sustained. Unfortunately, the extremely small number of cases in his study raises serious questions about the reliability of his findings. He had only ten respondents in Berkeley, California, 19 in Kansas City, and 22 in San Jose (Kerstetter, 1985:168-169). The technique, however, appears to be a viable one.

The Vera Institute (1989b) surveyed a sample of 371 citizens who had filed complaints with the New York City CCRB. Significantly, it found a much lower rate of satisfaction among those whose complaints were fully investigated (16%), compared with those who withdrew their complaints (62%), and those who accepted conciliation (59%). Vera concluded that "the investigative process itself has a significant negative influence" on citizen satisfaction. Dissatisfaction was associated with the length of time the complaint process took, the lack of contact with and information about the subject officer, and the final outcome. Not surprisingly, those whose complaints were substantiated were more satisfied than other complainants.

One of the important findings of the Vera study involved the conciliation option. Under the CCRB procedures, the complainant may be offered conciliation if the evidence is weak, the alleged misconduct not serious, and the subject officer does not have a long record of prior complaints (Vera, 1989b:3). Vera found that a minority of complainants (20%) desired severe punishment for the officer(s). Most (61%) had "moderate" objectives: an apology for themselves and/or a reprimand of the officer(s). The desire for a direct encounter with the subject officer(s) was "pervasive" and "significantly associated with complainant satisfaction" (Vera, 1989b:11).

The Vera study suggests a refinement of the objectives of civilian review. Many civilian review advocates conceptualize it in terms of a criminal trial, with a formal public hearing, presentation of evidence and cross-examination, and a formal adjudication. The Vera study suggests that evaluating the effectiveness of civilian review needs to be approached from the standpoint of a variety of possible procedures and outcomes, with each tailored to the seriousness of the alleged offense and the expressed desires of the complainant.

The literature on civilian review has, to date, neglected a large body of literature by social psychologists on the question of procedural justice. Lind and Tyler (1988) conclude that people who seek justice through some formal mechanism (e.g., the courts) are at least as concerned with the procedure itself as with the outcome. The result is not necessarily as important as the process of interaction—of getting a hearing and having a sense of being heard. This is consistent with the findings of the Vera study (1989b) of complainants in New York City. Future research on the effectiveness of civilian review needs to take into account the insights emerging from the work on procedural justice.

Review Board Determinations vs. Police Determinations

Another potential measure of effectiveness would be the extent to which the determinations made by civilians in a complaint process differ from the determinations made by the police department. This approach would be particularly relevant in Class II systems (Walker & Bumphus, 1991) where a board or civilian agency director reviews investigative reports completed by the police internal affairs unit. Several of the current civilian review procedures publish data that provide some suggestive, although not definitive, leads on this matter. In 1990, the San Diego Citizens' Review Board disagreed with internal affairs findings in only seven of 297 Category I incidents (the most serious allegations of misconduct). This represented 2.3 percent of all Category I cases. The Review Board disagreed with internal affairs in only three of 138 Category II allegations (or 2.1% of all cases) (San Diego, 1990). In New York City, the pattern of disagreement was far more complex. The CCRB disagreed with 98 recommendations of its investigative staff (composed of both sworn officers and non-sworn investigators). This represented 8.4 percent of the 1,153 completed investigations in 1990. It disagreed with ten findings of "substantiated," reducing them to some lesser category for which no discipline would be recommended (New York CCRB, 1990:17). The ten originally substantiated cases were from a total of between 150 and 200 substantiated cases. The reporting of the data in the CCRB's *Annual Report* is not clear on this point. The CCRB also disagreed with 65 findings of unsubstantiated," raising 28 (or 43%) to a finding of "substantiated." Only one other finding was raised to a finding of "substantiated." Thus, the CCRB raised the finding to a level at which formal discipline would occur in 29 of 98 disagreements (or 30%). In sum, the CCRB (which in 1990 did not include a majority of persons not employed by the police department) was more likely to recommend discipline than the investigative staff only rarely (slightly less than three percent of all completed investigations).

Several commentators have noted that civilian review procedures sustain citizen complaints at very low rates, rates that are not significantly higher than those reported by internal affairs units. The New York City CCRB substantiated only 3.8 percent of all complaints filed in 1988 and 2.8 percent in 1989. This appears to be an international phenomenon. Maguire (1991:187) found that the new Police Complaints Authority (PCA) substantiated only 8.2 percent of all fully investigated complaints, a rate that was "similar" to the previous and less independent procedure.

In some situations it may be possible to compare the record of the civilian complaint procedure with the police internal affairs unit. In some cities there is concurrent or overlapping jurisdiction over certain kinds of complaints. Hudson (1972) compared the activities of the Philadelphia Police Advisory Board (PAB) with the police internal affairs unit for several years in the 1960s. He found that the internal affairs unit was more likely to recommend discipline. Yet, this was a result of the fact that the two procedures were handling very different kinds of misconduct. Internal affairs generally handled corruption charges and violations of departmental policy. Such incidents are likely to involve less ambiguity about the facts of the case than are citizen complaints about excessive physical force or offensive language as to the facts—incidents that are often "swearing matches" that cannot be resolved through physical evidence or objective witnesses.

Several comments about these data are in order. First, they suggest that citizens do not substantially disagree with the judgment of police complaint investigators. This suggests that police officer fears that a civilian review process will be a "kangaroo court" are unfounded. At the same time it also suggests that civil rights leaders are likely to be disappointed that a civilian review procedure does not produce more findings of police misconduct. Second, the low rate of disagreement may be a result of the fact that the fact-finding is done by sworn officers. This would be a Class II system according to Walker and Bumphus (1991). The Citizens' Review Board has available to it only the information generated by the internal affairs investigation. The Review Board does have the power to request further investigation (San Diego, 1990), but the possibilities for covering up misconduct obviously remains

Finally, it should not be forgotten that in all but a handful of cities the ultimate disciplinary power remains with the police chief executive (Patterson, 1991:287-289). Civilian review procedures have the power to recommend disciplinary action. The effectiveness of a civilian review procedure, therefore, depends upon the extent to which such recommendations are accepted and acted upon. The most independent review procedure imaginable would be rendered irrelevant if most recommendations were rejected. The data from the San Francisco Office of Citizen Complaints (1991) is not encouraging on this point. According to the OCC's 1991 statistical report, the police chief did not impose any discipline in about one-third of the cases sustained by the OCC.

These data suggest a number of issues related to the effectiveness of civilian review. What is the rate at which recommendations are accepted by the chief executive? Assuming a relatively high rate of nonacceptance, what factors explain that pattern? Are there problems associated with the quality of the investigations and recommendations of the civilian review agency? Is there a highly antagonistic relationship between the civilian review agency and the chief executive? If so, is this antagonism the product of institutional conflict, particular personalities, or some other factors?

Civilian Review as a Policy-Making Agency

Some advocates of civilian review argue that the procedure can serve as a monitor or maker of police department policy. Maguire (1991:186, 192-193) defines this as the "feedback" function of civilian review. Only a few of the existing civilian review procedures in the United States have this function as part of their official role. Most are limited to the review of individual citizen complaints on a case-by-case basis. The Philadelphia Police Advisory Board (PAB), however, had the authority to make recommendations about general police policy (Coxe, 1965). The current civilian review procedures in Tucson, Arizona and Berkeley, California have similar authority (Walker & Bumphus, 1991). Possibly even more important, the Tucson Citizens' Police Advisory Committee has the authority to undertake investigations on its own initiative, without having to wait for a citizen to file a complaint.

Advocates of this particular role argue that it can serve an effective preventive role, making corrections in general police operations in a way that might reduce the number of complaints in the future (ACLU, 1992). An evaluation of this dimension of effectiveness could identify specific policy recommendations, determine whether they were implemented, and whether there was any reduction in complaints that might be attributed to the change.

Civilian Review as a Data Source

A recent manual on fighting police misconduct argues that a civilian review procedure could serve as an important source of data on police practices (ACLU, 1992). This addresses the traditional problem of the closed police bureaucracy and the difficulty in obtaining even the most rudimentary information about police practices, citizen complaints, and the disposition of complaints. Although researchers have had considerable success in recent years gaining access to police files on the use of deadly force (Fyfe, 1979; Geller & Karates, 1981), police departments have not been similarly forthcoming with respect to the use of physical force or other forms of misconduct. According to the proposed strategy (ACLU, 1992), the effectiveness of a civilian review procedure would be indirect. Instead of recommending discipline in particular cases, it would provide data that elected officials, community activists, and the news media could use to bring pressure on the police department to make needed changes. The strategy assumes that a civilian review agency would be less defensive about the implications of certain data and would be legally empowered to obtain and publish it.

Some already available data suggest how data generated by a civilian review agency could be used as a part of a strategy for improving police performance. One of the most important results of the Rodney King brutality case was a dramatic increase in public concern about police misconduct, as represented by official investigating commissions and investigative reporting by journalists.

Perhaps the single most important finding has been the fact that a small number of officers generate a disproportionate percentage of all complaints. This phenomenon had previously been documented by the U.S. Civil Rights Commission (1981). The Commission recommended that departments establish "early warning systems" to identify officers involved in an excessive number of citizen complaints and to take appropriate action to remedy the problem. The phenomenon of the "high complaint rate" officers (referred to colloquially as the "bad boys") has also been found in the Los Angeles police department (Independent Commission, 1991), the Los Angeles County Sheriff's Department (Kolts, 1992), Boston (1992), and Kansas City (*New York Times*, 1991).

A civilian review agency could generate such data on a routine basis, alerting both responsible police administrators and members of the public to the existence of problem-prone officers. There are certain problems with such a strategy that would have to be overcome. Police unions would oppose the identification of "problem" officers by name. They would have a valid claim that using unsubstantiated complaints for such identification would represent a form of punishment without adequate due process. This problem might be overcome if officers were identified by a code number (e.g., Officer #1, etc.). This would protect the privacy and due process rights of the individual officer, while at the same time alerting responsible officials and the public to the existence of certain problem officers. It would be useful to know, for example, whether there were many such officers or only a handful; whether the number of problem officers had declined over previous years; whether the number of complaints involving the seemingly worst officers was declining over previous years.

Data published by existing civilian review agencies already provide valuable data on patterns of police misconduct. The New York City Civilian Complaint Review Board (1990) confirms the fact that racial minority citizens and low-income neighborhoods are disproportionately represented among citizen complaints. As expected, younger officers are involved in more complaints than senior officers. Younger officers are more often assigned to patrol duty in high-crime areas and on the evening shift, assignments that are presumptively more likely to generate conflict-filled encounters between the police and citizens (Fyfe, 1981).

With respect to officer race, however, the New York City data indicated that officers were represented as the subject of complaints at rates equal to their presence in the department. This is consistent with Reiss' (1968; 1971) earlier finding that excessive use of force did not follow a clear pattern of racial discrimination—although they may have accumulated over time among low-income and racial minority males. The data also indicate that, with perhaps one exception, officers were no more likely to use force against citizens of one race compared with another. The exception was that Hispanic officers were involved in a higher rate of complaints from Hispanic citizens. Female officers, meanwhile, were the subject of complaints at only one-half the rate of their presence in the department. This finding is supported by the fact that in other departments female officers have not been identified as among those officers who are the subject of a high rate of complaints (Independent Commission, 1991). Subsequent research could be directed to investigating whether the low rate of complaints against female officers reflects gender-related differences in on-the-street behavior or some other causal factor.

Conclusions

For several decades, controversy over the concept of civilian review of the police has primarily involved the question of whether such a procedure should be established in a particular community. To a great extent, that question has been settled. Over two-thirds of the 50 largest cities in the United States have created some form of civilian review. These actions represent a legislative finding that the concept is an appropriate response to the problem of police misconduct.

The recent spread of civilian review introduces a new era in the history of this subject and raises a new set of questions. The important issues involve questions of effectiveness. What works? What kinds of systems are more effective than others? What kinds of procedures and resources are associated with success? How should success be measured? What kind of data is necessary for meaningful evaluations? This article has attempted to identify some of the problems facing any attempt to undertake a meaningful evaluation of the effectiveness of civilian review.

Notes

[1] A valuable but non-systematic collection of information on civilian review procedures is found in Association of Civilian Oversight of Law Enforcement (IACOLE), Compendium of Civilian Oversight Agencies (Evanston, IL, revised periodically). The Compendium is particularly valuable for information on civilian review procedures outside the United States. The data is summarized in Patterson (1991).

[2] The four new cities are Virginia Beach, VA; Seattle, WA; Denver, CO, and San Jose, CA. In 1992 the mayor of Boston also created a limited civilian review procedure by executive order. Author's notes and conversations.

[3] Because of the number of changes over the course of nearly 40 years (Kahn, 1975), the New York City CCRB presents an almost impossible situation with respect to effective starting date. The authors of the survey determined that the changes made in 1987 constituted an important turning point in the history of the agency.

[4] Kerstetter's categories are: civilian review, civilian input, and civilian monitor.

[5] On this point, there is some ambiguity regarding the powers of the Milwaukee Police and Fire Commission, the Baltimore Complaint Evaluation Board, and the Chicago Police Board.

[6] There is considerable literature on the early history of civilian review in Philadelphia (Terrill, 1988) and New York City (Kahn, 1975).

[7] These data are consistent with the findings of West's (1988) national survey conducted in 1987.

[8] This evidence consists largely of the author's telephone conversations with journalists and community activists.

[9] The assumption here is that more serious incidents, such as physical force, are more likely to be taken seriously by both complainant and investigators and more likely to involve physical evidence, such as injury requiring medical attention, that can help to verify the allegation. Less serious incidents, such as verbal abuse, are particularly difficult to verify.

[10] The Perez data is more readily available in Kerstetter (1985:162, 163, 168-169).

References

ACLU (1992). *Fighting Police Abuse: A Community Action Manual.* New York, NY: Author.

ACLU (1966). *Police Power and Citizens' Rights: The Case For an Independent Police Review Board.* New York, NY: Author.

ACLU-Southern California (1992). *The Call for Change Goes Unanswered.* Los Angeles, CA: Author.

Boston (1992). *Report of the Boston Police Department Management Review Committee.* Boston, MA: Office of the Mayor.

Boston Globe (1992). "Wave of Abuse Claims Laid to a Few Officers." (October 4).

Coxe, S. [Former Executive Director, Philadelphia ACLU] (1988). Interview with author.

Coxe, S. (1965). "The Philadelphia Police Advisory Board." *Law in Transition Quarterly* 2:179-185.

Crew, J. [Staff Counsel, Northern California ACLU] (1991). Interview with author.

Fyfe, J. (1981). "Who Shoots? A Look at Officer Race and Police Shooting." *Journal of Police Science and Administration*, 9:367-382.

Fyfe, J. (1979). "Administrative Interventions on Police Shooting Discretion. *Journal of Criminal Justice*, 7(Winter):309-323.

Garofalo, J. (1991). "Racially Motivated Crimes in New York City." In M. Lynch and E. Patterson (eds.), *Race and Criminal Justice*. New York, NY: Harrow and Heston.

Geller, W. and K. Karales (1981). *Split-Second Decisions*. Chicago, IL: Chicago Law Enforcement Study Group.

Goldsmith, A. (1991). *Complaints Against the Police: The Trend to External Review*. Oxford, England: Clarendon Press.

Gradison, M. [Former Executive Director Indiana ACLU] (1989). Interview with author.

Harris, L. (1992). "Public Solidly Favors Mixed Police/Civilian Review Boards." *Law Enforcement News*, (October 31, 1992).

Hudson, J. (1972). "Organizational Aspects of Internal and External Review of the Police." *Journal of Criminal Law, Criminology, and Police Science*, 63 (September):427-432.

Independent Commission on the Los Angeles Police Department (1991). *Report*. Los Angeles, CA: Author.

International Association for Civilian Oversight of Law Enforcement (1981). *Compendium of International Civilian Oversight Agencies*. Evanston, IL: Author.

Kahn, R. (1975). "Urban Reform and Police Accountability in New York City: 1950-1974." In R. Lineberry (ed.), *Urban Problems and Public Policy*. Lexington, MA: Lexington Books.

Kansas City, Office of Citizen Complaints (1983). *Annual Report*. Kansas City, MO: Author.

Kerstetter, W. (1985). "Who Disciplines the Police? Who Should?" In W. Geller (ed.), *Police Leadership in America: Crisis and Opportunity*. New York, NY: Praeger.

Kolts, J. (1992). *The Los Angeles County Sheriff's Department: A Report*. Los Angeles, CA: L.A. County Sheriffs Department.

Law Enforcement News (1992). "Denver Presses Ahead With High Powered Civilian Review Panel." (September 30).

Lind, E. and T. Tyler (1988). *The Social Psychology of Procedural Justice*. New York, NY: Plenum.

Littlejohn, E. (1981). "The Civilian Police Commission: A Deterrent of Police Misconduct." *University of Detroit Journal of Urban Law*, 59 (Fall):5-62.

Maguire, N. (1991). "Complaints Against the Police: The British Experience. In A. Goldsmith (ed.), *Complaints Against the Police: The Trend Toward External Review*. Oxford, England: Clarendon Press.

New York City, Civilian Complaint Investigative Bureau (1990). *Annual Report.* New York, NY: Author.

New York Civil Liberties Union (1993). *Civilian Review Agencies: A Comparative Study.* New York, NY: Author.

New York Civil Liberties Union (1990). *Police Abuse: The Need for Civilian Investigation and Oversight.* New York, NY: Author.

New York Times (1991a). "Police Attacks: Hard Crimes to Uncover, Let Alone Stop." (March 24):IV:4.

New York Times (1991b). "Complaints About Police Declining in New York." (March 27): B12.

New York Times (1991c). "Kansas City Police Go After Their 'Bad Boys.'" (September 10).

Perez, D. (1992). *Civilian Review of the Police.* (Advance copy of manuscript).

Perez, D. (1978). "Police Accountability: A Question of Balance." Berkeley, CA: Ph.D. Dissertation, University of California at Berkeley.

Patterson, W. (1991). "Police Accountability and Civilian Oversight of Policing: An American Perspective." In A. Goldsmith (ed.), *Complaints Against the Police: The Trend to External Review.* Oxford, England: Clarendon Press.

Police Chief (1964). "Civilian Review Boards" (Summer).

Police Executive Research Forum (1981). *Police Agency Handling of Citizen Complaints: A Model Policy Statement.* Washington, DC: Author.

Reiss, A. (1971). *The Police and the Public.* New Haven, CT: Yale University Press.

Reiss, A. (1968). "Police Brutality—Key Answers to Key Questions." *Transaction,* 5 (July-August): 10-19.

Ripston, R. [Executive Director Southern California ACLU] (1991). Interview with author.

San Diego, Citizens' Review Board (1990). *Annual Report.* San Diego, CA: Citizens' Review Board.

San Francisco (1991). *Office of Citizen Complaints: 1991 Year-End Statistical Report.* San Francisco, CA: The Police Commission.

Sherman, L. (1987). *Repeat Calls to the Police.* Washington, DC: Crime Control Institute.

Sherman, L. and B. Glick (1984). *The Quality of Police Arrest Statistics.* Washington, DC: The Police Foundation.

Siegel, N. [Executive Director, New York Civil Liberties Union] (1991). Interview with author.

Taylor, K. [Executive Director Washington (State) ACLU] (1991). Interview with author.

Terrill. R. (1991). "Civilian Oversight of the Police Complaints Process in the United States: Concerns, Developments, and More Concerns." In A. Goldsmith (ed.), *Complaints Against the Police.* Oxford, England: Clarendon Press.

Terrill, R. (1988). "Police Accountability in Philadelphia: Retrospects and Prospects." *American Journal of Police,* 7:79-99.

U.S. Civil Rights Commission (1981). *Who Is Guarding the Guardians?* Washington, DC: U.S. Government Printing Office.

U.S. Department of Justice (1991). *Criminal Victimization in the United States, 1989.* Washington, DC: U.S. Government Printing Office.

U.S. Department of Justice (1977). *Public Opinion About Crime.* Washington, DC: U.S. Government Printing Office.

Vera Institute (1989a). *The Processing of Complaints Against Police in New York City: The Perception and Attitudes of Line Officers.* New York, NY: Vera Institute (September).

Vera Institute (1989b). *Processing Complaints Against Police in New York City: The Complainant's Perspective.* New York, NY: Vera Institute (January).

Vera Institute (1988). *Processing Complaints Against Police: The Civilian Complaint Review Board—Executive Summary.* New York, NY: Vera Institute (January).

Walker, S. (1992). *Update: The Current Status of Civilian Review.* Omaha, NE: University of Nebraska at Omaha, unpublished notes.

Walker, S. (1990). In *Defense of American Liberties: A History of the ACLU.* New York, NY: Oxford University Press.

Walker, S. and V. Bumphus (1991). *Civilian Review of the Police: A National Survey of the 50 Largest Cities, 1991.* Omaha, NE: University of Nebraska at Omaha.

West, P. (1988). *Police Complaint Procedures in the USA and in England and Wales: Historical and Contemporary Issues.* Ann Arbor, MI: Unpublished M.S. Thesis, Michigan State University. University Microfilms International.

Westley, W. (1970). *Violence and the Police.* Cambridge, MA: MIT Press.

Whitaker, G. (1982). *Basic Issues in Policing.* Washington, DC: U.S. Government Printing Office.

Police Leadership and the Reconciliation of Police-Minority Relations

Kenneth Aaron Betsalel
University of North Carolina at Asheville

Despite some genuine changes in American policing in the past twenty-five years, police-minority relations continue to be a source of concern in many communities throughout the nation (National Minority Advisory Council, 1982; U.S. Department of Justice, 1986; Jackson, 1989; Sunderman and Keyes, 1989). One way to conceptualize the problem of police-minority relations is as the tension between the minority (black and Hispanic) concern with equal protection of the law and the police concern with crime control and the maintenance of order (Bayley and Mendelsohn, 1969; Cooper, 1980). From the minority perspective, police have often been viewed as an "occupying force" more concerned with restricting their freedom than in providing service; from the police point of view, minority neighborhoods have not always been supportive of their effort to "right" crime (Groves and Rossi, 1970; Hahn, 1971; Radelet, 1986:193-194). The result is often conflict and mistrust between minorities and the police.

Based on my study of city politics and governmental responses to crime in San Jose, California between 1948 and 1988 (Betsalel, 1983; forthcoming), this article uses the example of Police Chief Joseph D. McNamara to focus on the role of police leadership in reconciling the conflicting interests that are associated with police-minority relations.[1] The approach taken is speculative in nature. This essay makes no pretense of being "scientific" in the sense that hypotheses are rigorously tested and verified. Instead, it is intended as a thought piece that stresses the importance of leadership in shaping the values that help guide the actions of police officers. I will conclude that while police leadership may not be the only factor that contributes to more cooperative police-minority relations, the philosophy of the police administrator does have the capacity to influence the kind of department values that either contribute to or lessen police-minority conflict.

Without dynamic statesman-like police leadership, according to Sherman (1985:462), it is unlikely that police will be able to succeed in improving the quality of police work or the life of the city. By "statesman," Sherman means "a leader of democracy, someone who can transcend the current values of the day and lead both police and the public into accepting a better set of values and strategies for policing." Similarly, Reiss (1985:68) characterizes the dynamic police leader as one who not only responds to the environment but helps shape it for the better.

In short, a police chief needs to be a political leader, not in a narrowly defined self-interested way (the image of a cynical, cigar-chomping, back-room, deal-making, vote-getting "pol") but rather in the more sober tradition of the political leader as someone who is deeply concerned with the welfare of the community and all of its inhabitants—citizen and stranger alike. It was in this sense that the German sociologist Max Weber (1946:128) explained that a leader needs both "passion and perspective": the passion—indeed courage—to enter the hard world of public life, and the perspective to use political power wisely.

Leadership (Selznick, 1957:37,62) helps "define the ends of group existence" by "reconcil[ing] internal strivings" of organizations with the "environmental pressures" for change. Selznick can be interpreted as arguing that, because of their role as "mediators" or what may be thought of as arbiters of conflicting organizational and group demands, leaders—whether they be police chiefs, corporate executives or university presidents—have the potential to transform organizations into institutions that are worthy of public respect and support. McFarland (1969:217) further suggests that by "redefining conflict situations" in order to resolve what at first may appear to be incompatible value-demands, leaders act as "independent forces" in history to bring about what he characterizes as "socio-political innovation."

In other words, by exercising independent judgment and reconciling conflicting value-demands, leadership can help facilitate social progress.

San Jose

Prior to the arrival of Police Chief Joseph McNamara in 1976, San Jose's police-minority relations were in continuous turmoil and crisis (ABC News, 1985; Geilhufe, 1979). The U.S. Civil Rights Commission, Western Regional Office (1980:9) reported:

> Spokespersons from the [minority] community alleged widespread mistrust and fear of San Jose police . . . There were many allegations of abuse of authority and excessive force. The situa-

> tion was heated and tense. The response of city officials to community grievances and recommendations was alleged to be inadequate. A pattern of civilian fatalities by police over a 7-year period coupled with daily confrontations with law enforcement officers led citizens to demand change. The community believed that police officers were seldom disciplined and that the department's internal investigations unit was a closed shop which protected officers. The department's administration was viewed as ineffective.

These findings echoed earlier government reports that minority community leaders believed that the San Jose police department had a "double standard" of justice—one for minorities and one for everybody else (U.S. Commission on Civil Rights, 1970:12; Citizen's Ad Hoc Committee, 1972).

According to Wilson (1972:69), a major cause of police-minority conflict is the "incompatibility" of the organizational mission of the police to suppress crime with the democratic aspirations of minorities to be at liberty "like all persons to come and go as they please." As he put it: "So long as crime and disorder are disproportionately to be found among young lower-class males, and so long as blacks remain over-represented (though by no means identical with) such groups, blacks—especially young ones—and the police are going to be adversaries" (1972:69). In essence, the conflict between minorities and police from this perspective is between competing value claims of individual liberty versus the need for social order.

Many experts on police in the 1960s and 1970s were doubtful about the prospect of meaningful improvement in police-minority relations. Doig (1968:396-397) represented such a view when he wrote in the pages of the *Public Administration Review* that proposals for police reform

> . . . confront the prospect of being ignored by the police or slowly ground to pieces in the bureaucratic system . . . Even a police commissioner and mayor dedicated to change will generally lack the time and energy to ensure that proposals become more than paper directives—that they actually affect the behavior of the individual precinct sergeant and the patrolman on the beat.

Levy (1969:68), observing the situation in Detroit in 1969, was even more blunt about the possibility of improving police-minority relations when he argued that higher police pay, police training programs or police-community dialogues and the like would do "little to stop the pattern of police discrimination and brutality against Negroes and other minorities in America's urban ghettos." Levy concluded: "The problem is one of a set of values and attitudes and a pattern of anti-black behavior, socialized within and reinforced by the police system."

More recently, Scheingold (1984:137) has argued that the "politics of law and order" with its emphasis on the values of crime control has "re-created a climate of opinion and a balance of organizational forces that is inimical to community service ideas and is likely to drive crime-attack policies back toward suspect priorities and abusive police practices . . ." All of which, if true, would no doubt increase conflict between police and minorities.

Yet despite these admittedly gloomy predictions and the fact that on a national basis blacks and Hispanics continue to be less satisfied with police services than are whites (U.S. Department of Justice, 1988:135), police-minority relations in the metropolitan city of San Jose appear to have improved markedly since the arrival of Chief McNamara.

Evidence of this improvement can be measured in terms of police responsiveness to minority community concerns, the opinions expressed by minority community leaders and by knowledgeable observers both inside and outside the police department, and editorial and media coverage. For example, a U.S. Civil Rights Commission report (1980:iii) stated that the effort led by Chief McNamara to improve police-community relations in San Jose might well serve as a model for other cities.

Central to the positive shift in police-minority relations in San Jose was a widely perceived transformation in the prevailing police ethic from an emphasis on strict crime control or what Wilson (1968:171) refers to as a "legalistic style," to a more crime-prevention, community-service orientation or what Kelling (1988a:2) and other scholars such as Goldstein (1987) have begun to refer to as "community policing."

Evidence for this change includes a proliferation of police programs designed to win minority community support and an apparent change in the prevailing police attitude toward law enforcement. Although difficult to measure, community policing is associated with a qualitative change in prevailing police values that is more important than technical or programmatic changes (which can be easily counted). As Wasserman and Moore (1988:5) explain, community policing

> . . . reflects a set of values, rather than a technical orientation toward the police function. It reflects a concern with the quality of police service delivery, the relationship between the police and the community, and the relationship within the police agency between management and employees. As opposed to the more traditional perspective of professional crime-fighting . . . community policing emphasizes service output, the quality of results, and the impact of police service on the state of urban living.

While San Jose police officers still recognize their responsibility to maintain law and order, they have earned the reputation of being less aggressive, confrontational and legalistic, and more willing to accommodate a wider and more pluralistic notion of what that order is. To argue that there has been marked improvement in San Jose's police-minority relations is not to say that the relationship has reached a state of utopia, that there are no outspoken minority critics of the police, that older and more dissident factions do not still exist within the police department that opposed the shift toward a more community-service, responsive style of policing, or, that police tactics from time to time do not draw them into controversial situations with the minority community. According to almost all knowledgeable observers, however, a mood of 'urban ease" and sense of respect and cooperation has begun to develop between the police and the minority community as a direct result of police leadership's effort in this area.

Police administrators prior to McNamara were unable to successfully accommodate minority community demands with police rank-and-file concerns. Undoubtedly, this was in part due to the times in which these efforts were made, because throughout the 1960s and 1970s, conflict between police and minorities reached epidemic proportions nationwide. But this national trend does not explain why conflict between police and the minority community in San Jose went unabated well into the 1970s and showed no meaningful improvement until McNamara's administration. According to knowledgeable observers, the failure of police-minority relations in San Jose was in large part due to a failure of leadership (U.S. Civil Rights Commission, 1980:10).

While McNamara's success in improving police-minority relations drew upon the efforts of his predecessors and the work of many individuals within the department, it is also a result of his leadership style and policing philosophy. His was a philosophy that was able to incorporate police officers' bureaucratic concerns with efficiency, professionalism and personal security, while at the same time respond to the minority community's democratic yearning for equality of treatment and personal liberty. McNamara's organizational leadership had the effect of transforming and elevating police and minorities into citizens worthy of each other's respect. Because McNamara has succeeded where others have failed, and because the relationship between police and minorities is so essential to the quality of life in our cities, it is instructive to examine his philosophy of policing and leadership style more closely.

Basic Principles

While it is difficult to distinguish between the means and ends of police administration, for analytic purposes the following basic principles are fundamental to McNamara's policing philosophy and a key to understanding his effort in reconciling the competing value demands of minorities and the police.

First, unlike his predecessors, McNamara, who received his Ph.D. in public administration from Harvard University, has a clearly articulated policing philosophy. Like Skolnick (1967:245), he believes that police officers are more than "efficient administrators of criminal law,' they are legal and moral actors as well. In other words, police officers have a responsibility to remain within the bounds of law while at the same time exercising their discretion and good judgment. This means that the law cannot be applied in a mechanical or technocratic way but has to take into account context and often ambiguous and uncertain circumstances, and that policing requires thinking and moral courage at least as much, if not more, than it does physical strength and the use of brute force. Because of this it is critically important for police leadership to communicate to both the public and rank-and-file police exactly what is expected: in this case, an "attitude of public service and protection" as opposed to strict crime control and legalistic law enforcement (U.S. Commission on Civil Rights, 1980:16).

Second, in order to improve the quality of police-minority relations, officers must come to understand rather than acting in a callous or indifferent manner toward the sometimes tragic aspects of life they encounter. Muir (1977:3) has written that in order for police officers to become true professionals they need to intellectually "grasp the nature of human suffering." It is toward a similar end that McNamara attempts to educate his officers regarding the importance of empathy. His own experience as a young patrol officer in New York's Harlem had affected him deeply, and by sharing his personal experiences, as well as through training programs in social and cultural awareness, McNamara believes his officers will come to develop a better understanding of the people they police and the conditions under which they live.

Third, as the foundation of good police work is based on encouraging close and cooperative community relations and since so much of police work involves contact with citizens in minority neighborhoods, this basic principle is even more important to establish. In order to achieve minority community support, McNamara advocates an "open-door" policy and he goes into the community himself to talk to minority leaders and organizations about his policing philosophy. Gaining the support of the minority community also means ensuring that all citizen-initiated complaints against the police are handled fairly, promptly and in an open and straightforward manner. (McNamara made the controversial decision to move the Bureau of Internal Affairs to a location outside the department and hire a bilingual civilian to handle the complaint process.) Maintaining the minority community's trust also calls for a genuine sense of openness and honesty on the chiefs part—even to the point of admitting a mistake or error in judgment, particularly in the use of deadly force. Previous discrimination against minorities has to be recognized and affirmative action measures taken to "make up for" past practices.

Fourth is the principle that good police-minority relations are built not only on a faithful adherence to the dictates of law but also by the manner in which the police choose to define their central tasks. The dominant image of the police in the 1950s and 1960s was that of professional crime fighters. As already suggested, this self definition placed an emphasis on aggressive street behavior, patrol techniques and a strict legalistic interpretation of the law. According to the crime control model of policing, the patrol officer's duty was to vigorously and uncompromisingly enforce the law against all major and minor lawbreakers wherever possible. McNamara places a different emphasis on the role of police in society by stressing that the police must work *with* the community and the community with the police in identifying problem areas and possible solutions. In effect, this philosophy holds that the police and community must enter into a reciprocal relationship in terms of sharing knowledge and power. In return, police will gain respect, cooperation and the kind of knowledge and insight into the nature of the community that will enable them to do their job better, while at the same time minorities will recognize that police are genuinely concerned with what they have to say and with the special problems they confront in their neighborhoods. This last point of sharing "knowledge and power," according to Lee P. Brown (a former San Jose police officer and now Police Commissioner of New York City), is the essence of community policing (1985; also see Alpert and Dunham, 1988 on the closely related concept of neighborhood policing).

Fifth, while McNamara recognizes that economy of scale prevents the San Jose police department from decentralizing its operation by establishing "storefront offices" or neighborhood precincts, he urges officers to get out of their patrol cars and become better acquainted with the people they serve. Following up on earlier concepts initiated by his predecessors, he also advocates extending district assignments, and the concept of team policing. As McNamara explained his philosophy of community policing to noted author Charles Silberman (1978:204-205) in his study of crime and the criminal justice system in the United States:

> [I]mproving police-community relations is not a goal that can be achieved through public relations campaigns, nor is it a task to be delegated to a specialized staff division; it is what policing is all about . . . Most communities are underutilizing their police departments . . . members of the public have a role to play in crime control and they are far more likely to play that role if the cop is someone they know and trust instead of a brusque stranger.

Finally, McNamara argues that the success of police-minority relations ultimately rests not on novel programs and ideas but on the ability of police leadership to be believed in by the community and to be taken seriously by rank-and-file officers. This often means that police leadership has to take principled positions in working with police unions. Thus, police leadership has to make it clear to the rank-and-file that while the chief may understand the difficulty of their job, the discipline of the profession requires that good police-minority relations never be compromised for the sake of morale or internal police department harmony.

In essence, McNamara's philosophy centers on teaching the importance of being "democratic police officers;" that the duty of the police is to serve and protect the public, not to make the public conform to a rigidly conceived notion of law and order. The police have to represent authority without being authoritarian; to respect the rights of a free people while themselves living and working within a system of checks and balances and constitutional government. In the end, these are the universal values police officers are sworn to uphold rather than the more particularist interests associated with professional crime fighting. "In representing the law," Berkley (1969:213) has written, the police officer "represents our code of civilization" and therefore must incorporate and personify these essential values.

As to the question of how representative McNamara's police leadership is in facilitating better police-minority relations, it is difficult to say. American cities and their police departments vary a great deal. However, according to Skolnick and Bayley (1986:7, 220), who observed policing in six American cities (as diverse as Santa Ana, California; Houston, Texas; and Newark, New Jersey), police leadership is the single most important factor in the development of innovative policing strategies. Similarly, Kelling (1988a, 1988b) and his colleagues at Harvard University argue that a new generation of progressive police chiefs are helping to lead a "quiet revolution" in American police-community relations.

By acting from a principled position, McNamara exemplifies what James McGregor Burns (1978:4, 461) has referred to as "transforming" or "moral" leadership: the kind of leadership that does not eliminate the complex conflicts inherent in the value demands of democracy and bureaucracy but instead attempts to teach the kind of moral strength and reliance on the rule of law that over time will empower both police and minority citizens to reconcile those competing value claims for themselves.

Conclusion

To the extent that police leadership can help elevate police-minority relations to a more cooperative level—one that replaces fear with trust—police leadership can be viewed as helping to forge a "new social contract," a concept reminiscent of that of the political theorist Rousseau (1712- 1778) who explained:

> As a result of the contract [citizens] find themselves in a situation preferable in real terms to that which prevailed before; instead of alienation, they have profitably exchanged an uncertain and precarious life for a better and more secure one; they

> have exchanged natural independence for freedom, the power to destroy others for the enjoyment of their own security; they have exchanged their own strength which others might overcome for a right which the social union makes invincible (*The Social Contract: Book II*, Ch. 4).

Of course, the police leader in a democratic society is not the only actor who transmits the values associated with respect for the law and, for lack of a better phrase, "good citizenship;" school teachers, clergy, parents and others in positions of authority all play their part in socializing core values or what the ancient Greeks called *paideia*. But it is only the police leader who has the opportunity, indeed responsibility, to apply those lessons to the problems associated with police-minority relations. And while police leadership is not the only factor contributing to the reconciliation of police-minority relations (the work of courts, city councils, media, and training officers no doubt all play a part), the chief's philosophy of policing can make the difference between the kind of values that exacerbate conflict and those that tend to reinforce cooperation in police-community relations.

Notes

Research for this article was financed in part by grant number 78-NI-AX-0096 from the National Institute of Justice, U.S. Department of Justice and by a Henry Robert Brandon Fund Fellowship from the University of California-Berkeley. A Summer Faculty Fellowship from Southwest Missouri State University made final preparations for this article possible. The author would also like to thank Daniel B. Cornfield, Herbert Jacob, Norman Jacobson, Eugene C. Lee, William K. Muir, Jr., and Jerome H. Skolnick for comments on an earlier version of this article. Of course, none of these individuals or institutions bears responsibility for the interpretation and conclusions expressed here.

[1] The empirical observations of San Jose's police-minority relations are based on more than 45 in-depth interviews with San Jose police and city officials (including interviews with three police chiefs, eight of the eleven mayors, and three of the five city managers who served in San Jose during the period of my field work); minority community leaders (including past directors of the Mexican-American Community Service Association, Casa Libra, and La Causa Unida); and local knowledgeable observers (including journalists, editorial writers and academicians). Field work also involved riding along with police in minority neighborhoods; attending city council meetings on occasions when issues relating to police-minority relations were under discussion; analysis of relevant documents such as government reports (including more than 120 open-ended interviews conducted between 1976 and 1979 by the Western Regional Office of the United States Civil Rights Commission on San Jose's police-community relations); Peace Officers Association (POA) newspapers, police department memorandums, and minority community organizing materials. In instances where either fact or interpretation is based solely on interviews, attempts were made to triangulate findings.

References

ABC World News Tonight (1985). "Police Brutality." Two-part special, July 23-24. Peter Jennings (NYC), with Jack Smith reporting.

Alpert, G. and R. Dunham (1988). *Policing Multi-Ethnic Neighborhoods.* New York, NY: Greenwood Press.

Bayley, D. and H. Mendelsohn (1969). *Minorities and the Police: Confrontation in America.* New York, NY: The Free Press.

Berkley, G. (1969). *The Democratic Policeman.* Boston, MA: Beacon Press.

Betsalel, K. (1983). "San Jose: Crime and the Politics of Growth." In A. Heinz, H. Jacob and R. Lineberry (eds.), *Crime in City Politics.* New York, NY: Longman.

________ (forthcoming). "The Police Shooting of Danny Travino and the Politics of Police-Minority Relations in San Jose." In D. Montjano (ed.), *Essays On Chicano Politics and Society.* Albuquerque, NM: University of New Mexico Press.

Burns, J. (1978). *Leadership.* New York, NY: Harper and Row.

Brown, L. (1985). "Police-Community Power Sharing." In W. Geller (ed.), *Police Leadership in America.* New York, NY: Praeger.

Citizen's Ad Hoc Committee (1972). *Final Report of the Ad Hoc Committee on the Policies and Procedures of the Police Department.* City of San Jose, California.

Cooper, J. (1980). *The Police and the Ghetto.* Port Washington, New York: Kennikat Press.

Doig, J. (1968). "Police Problems, Proposals and Strategies for Change." *Public Administration Review,* 28: 393-430.

Geithufe, N. (1979). *Chicanos and the Police: A Study of the Politics of Ethnicity in San Jose, California.* The Society for Applied Anthropology Monograph Number 13, Washington, D.C.

Goldstein, H. (1977). *Policing A Free Society.* Cambridge, MA: Ballinger.

________ (1987). "Toward Community-Oriented Policing: Potential, Basic Requirements and Threshold Questions." *Crime and Delinquency,* 33 (1): 6-30.

Groves, W. and P. Rossi (1970). "Police Perceptions of a Hostile Ghetto." *American Behavioral Scientist,* 13:727-44.

Hahn, H. (1971). "Ghetto Assessments of Police Protection and Authority." *Law and Society Review,* 6: 183-194.

Jackson, D. (1989) "Police Embody Racism To My People." *New York Times,* January 23.

Kelling, G. (1988a). "Police and Communities: The Quiet Revolution." *Perspectives On Policing,* No. 1. U.S. Department of Justice, National Institute of Justice.

_________ and M. Moore (1988b). "From Political to Reform to Community: The Evolving Strategy of Police." In J. Greene and S. Mastrofski (eds.), *Community Policing: Rhetoric or Reality.* New York, NY: Praeger.

Levy, B. (1968). "Cops in the Ghetto: A Problem of the Police System." *American Behavioral Scientist* (March-April): 31-34.

McFarland, A. (1969). *Power and Leadership in Pluralist Systems.* Stanford, CA: Stanford University Press.

Muir, W., Jr. (1977). *Police: Street Corner Politicians.* Chicago, IL: University of Chicago Press.

National Minority Advisory Council on Criminal Justice (1982). *The Inequality of Justice: A Report on Clime and the Administration of Justice in the Minority Community.* Washington, DC: U.S. Department of Justice.

Radelet, L. (1986). *The Police and the Community,* 4th ed. New York, NY: Macmillan.

Reiss, A., Jr. (1985). "Shaping and Serving the Community: The Role of the Police Chief Executive." In W. Geller (ed.), *Police Leadership in America.* New York, NY: Praeger.

Scheingold, S. (1984). *The Politics of Law and Order.* New York, NY: Longman.

Selznick, P. (1957). *Leadership in Administration: A Sociological Interpretation.* New York, NY: Harper & Row.

Sherman, L. (1985). "The Police Executive As Statesman." In W. Geller (ed.), *Police Leadership In America.* New York, NY: Praeger.

Silberman, C. (1978). *Criminal Violence, Criminal Justice.* New York, NY: Random House.

Skolnick, J. (1966). *Justice Without Trial: Law Enforcement in a Democratic Society.* New York, NY: John Wiley & Sons.

_________ and D. Bayley (1986). *The New Blue Line: Police Innovation in Six American Cities.* New York, NY: The Free Press.

Sunderman, G. and R. Keyes (1989). "Black Leaders Say Police Using Too Much Force." *News-Leader,* January 6. Springfield, Missouri.

United States Department of Justice (1986). *Annual Report of the Community Relations Service.* Washington, DC: author.

_________ (1988). *Sourcebook of Criminal Justice Statistics, 1987.* Washington DC: Bureau of Justice Statistics, U.S. Government Printing Office.

United States Commission on Civil Rights (1970). *Mexican-Americans and the Administration of Justice in the Southwest.* Washington, DC: author.

———— (1980). *Police-Community Relations in San Jose.* A Staff Report of the Western Regional Office of the U.S. Commission on Civil Rights. Washington, DC: author.

Wasserman, R. and M. Moore (1988). "Values In Policing." *Perspectives on Policing* No. 8. U.S. Department of Justice, National Institute of Justice.

Weber, M. (1946). *From Max Weber: Essays in Sociology.* Translated and edited by H. Gerth and C. Mills. New York, NY: Oxford University Press.

Wilson, J. (1968). *Varieties of Police Behavior: The Management of Law and Order in Eight Communities.* Cambridge, MA: Harvard University Press.

———— (1972). "The Police in the Ghetto." In R. Steadman (ed.), *The Police and the Community.* Baltimore, MD: The Johns Hopkins University Press.

Section II

Legal and Policy Issues

Introduction

Two interrelated sets of factors that strongly affect police management are legal issues and policy issues. Obviously, police organizations operate within legal environments—what may not be so obvious is the complexity of these legal environments. But consider the range of legal considerations and constraints that police departments must deal with: (1) changing state criminal codes (e.g., new laws prohibiting stalking); (2) changing local ordinances (e.g., newly enacted curfews for juveniles); (3) statutory changes in criminal procedure (e.g., authorization for misdemeanor probable cause arrests in spousal assault situations); (4) changes in police authority and procedure wrought by appeals court decisions, including those of the U.S. Supreme Court (e.g., the *Garner* decision affecting police use of deadly force); (5) changes in regulatory law that affect such police administrative activities as hiring, working conditions, and retirement (e.g., the recently enacted *Americans With Disabilities Act*); and (6) the threat of lawsuits emanating from the expansion of police civil liability.

Among the most significant policy issues facing contemporary police organizations are those concerning (1) the use of force, especially deadly force, (2) high-speed and pursuit driving, and (3) handling of domestic violence. These aspects of policing share several common characteristics: they involve substantial risk of physical harm to the parties involved; they may ultimately generate both criminal trials and civil lawsuits; and they are of intense concern to the general public.

Because of the risks involved and the high degree of concern, police departments are put under intense pressure to effectively manage their responses to such incidents. They are also constrained by legal developments, scrutinized by the media, influenced by various interest groups, and watched carefully by their own employees. Managing their organizations' responses to these kinds of high-profile issues is among the toughest and most important responsibilities of police executives.

The three articles in this section are directly concerned with the impact of legal and policy issues on police management. First, Vic Kappeler and Rolando del Carmen examine the civil liability of municipalities and police agencies. Readers should recognize that a range of individuals and entities might be found among the defendants in a civil action arising over police action, including: (1) individual police officers; (2) police supervisors, trainers, and managers; (3) police *agencies;* (4) local governments; and (5) state governments. This article focuses specifically on the liability of local police agencies and their host municipal governments. As the authors note, it has become increasingly common for these entities to be included as defendants in lawsuits, largely because they usually have deeper pockets (i.e., more money) than individual officers or their individual superiors.

Kappeler and del Carmen focus on agency and government liability for *official policy.* Basically, they report that police departments and their governments may be held liable if their written policies or unwritten customs and practices cause or permit individuals to be wrongfully harmed by police action or inaction. Importantly, although individual police officials may sometimes prevail with a "good faith" defense, this kind of defense is not available to police agencies or municipalities. Consequently, the authors recommend "constant policy review and ongoing supervision, particularly in view of the possibility that liability may be imposed not only because the agency policymakers knew, but also that they 'should have known' about the existence of unconstitutional policies and practices."

In the next article, Sam Walker and Lorie Fridell explore the impact of the U.S. Supreme Court's 1985 *Garner* decision on the deadly force policies of the 100 largest American cities. What they find is extremely interesting and runs counter to the conventional wisdom about court decisions and police administration. Almost 70% of the surveyed departments did *not* have to change their policies post-*Garner,* because their deadly force policies were already as restrictive, or more restrictive, than the decision's requirements.

Walker and Fridell argue that in this policy area, and perhaps in others, the police profession was out in front of the Supreme Court, not vice versa. The court, in essence, was merely sanctifying what had already become a standard within policing. Arguably, this speaks well for the advancing maturity of the police profession (although, of course, these restrictive deadly force policies may have been more the result of public and political pressure than far-sighted police leadership). Also, their finding may bespeak a new relationship between police organizations and appeals courts, in which the courts can refer more to accepted professional practice and rely less on the imposition of new, judicially invented practices.

In the third article of this section, "Developing Police Policy," Geoffrey Alpert and William Smith take a very careful and analytical look at the applicability of written directives and other forms of organizational control to different facets of policing. They offer two useful conceptual tools: a typology of risk categories and a continuum of policy control. In the typology, they distinguish between police activities that occur with high and low frequency and those that incur high- and low-risk exposure. High-frequency/high-risk situations (e.g., pursuit driving) and low-frequency/high-risk situations (e.g., deadly force) would seem to require the strictest controls, whereas low-risk situations may necessitate less formal control and permit more officer discretion.

With their policy control continuum, Alpert and Smith advance the discussion beyond a simple either/or debate over the desirability of strict formal controls. They demonstrate that some kinds of situations demand strict controls (e.g., use of force) while others require only summary guidance (e.g., telephone contacts). In the middle, though, are situations in which police officers need both guidance and discretion, such as in the handling of domestic disputes. In these kinds of situations, the authors advocate the use of structured guidelines that mandate certain procedures while permitting officers to utilize their skills and experience in seeking just and fair outcomes. Besides offering these suggestions, Alpert and Smith also point out that we actually have very little empirical evidence on which to base decisions about how best to control police use of discretion in order to maximize the accomplishment of police goals and objectives. Until we develop such evidence, we will probably continue to witness heated debates between those who advocate strict formal and top-down controls over police discretion and those who favor more informal and bottom-up controls.

Municipalities and Police Agencies as Defendants: Liability for Official Policy

Rolando V. del Carmen
Sam Houston State University

Victor E. Kappeler
Central Missouri State University

Government agencies may be sued and held liable under state tort law or 42 U.S.C. § 1983. In a typical § 1983 action against a city or agency, the plaintiff makes the following allegations: (1) that there is or was a policy; (2) that the policy was promulgated by the city or by the agency's policymaker; (3) that the policy caused the injury to the plaintiff; and (4) that the injury constituted a violation of plaintiff s constitutional rights.

States and state agencies generally cannot be sued under §§ 1983 because they enjoy sovereign immunity (which can be waived) under the Eleventh Amendment to the Constitution. The Eleventh Amendment provides: "The Judicial power of the United States shall not be construed to extend to any suit in law or equity, commenced or prosecuted against one of the United States by Citizens of another State, or by Citizens or Subjects of any Foreign state." This does not imply that state officials are immune from liability. Sovereign immunity extends only to the state itself and its agencies; state officials, like local officials, may be sued and held liable for what they do in their *personal* capacities. In a recent case, however, the Court held that state officials cannot be sued in their official capacities under § 1983 because such lawsuits are, in effect, lawsuits against the state (*Will v. Michigan Department of State Police*, 1989).[1]

Local agencies once enjoyed sovereign immunity in § 1983 cases, but in 1978 the Court decided that local agencies could be held liable under § 1983 for what their employees do, thus depriving local governments of the sovereign immunity barrier (*Monell v. Department of Social Services*, 1978). This change is partly responsible for the upsurge in liability cases against local police departments because now plaintiffs know that if the officer is too poor to pay, the agency may be held liable, if the violation can be attributed in some way to the agency. Some courts have held that although the agency is not civilly responsible for every act of a supervisor, the higher the supervisor's rank, the greater the chances of agency liability. For example, an agency is less likely to be found liable for the decision of a police sergeant than it is for decisions and policies promulgated by a police chief.

Liability for "Official Policy"

The Court held in *Monell* (1978:690) that municipal liability may be imposed for conduct that "implements or executes a policy statement, ordinance, regulation, or decision officially adopted and promulgated by municipal officers," or if such conduct results from "custom" even though such custom has not received formal approval through official decision-making channels. Agency or municipal liability generally ensues if the violation stems from "official policy." What, then, is "official policy?" The answer is unclear and has been the subject of court decisions that are difficult to reconcile.

At the risk of oversimplification, but in the interest of clarity, a working definition given by the Fifth Circuit Court of Appeals in the case of *Bennett v. City of Slidell* (1984:862) may be used. In that case the court said that official policy is:

1. A policy statement, ordinance, regulation, or decision that is officially adopted and promulgated by the municipality's lawmaking officers or by an official to whom the lawmakers have delegated policymaking authority or

2. A persistent, widespread practice of city officials or employees which, although not authorized by officially adopted and promulgated policy, is so common and well settled as to constitute a custom that fairly represents municipal policy. Actual or constructive knowledge of such custom must be attributable to the governing body of the municipality or to an official to whom that body had delegated policymaking authority.

This definition invites two observations. One is that for a policy to be official it must be officially adopted and promulgated by the municipality's lawmaking officers or by an official to whom lawmakers have delegated policymaking authority. Such a policy may be in the form of law, written regulations, directives, or policy statements of high executive officials (*Grandstaff v. City of Borger,* 1985). Not every police supervisor comes under this category. In a recent case, the United States Supreme Court said that the determination of which officials have final policymaking authority is a question of state and local law and not a question of fact for a judge or jury to decide (*City of St. Louis v. Praprotnik*, 1988). At least one court has found that a police chief is "one whose acts or edicts may fairly be said to represent official policy" (*Bordanaro v. McLeod*, 1989:1157).

The second observation is that a "custom," although unwritten, may constitute official policy. By definition, a "custom" implies that it has not been officially adopted or promulgated by policymakers, but it may be so common, widespread, and well-settled that it can be said to represent official policy. This is a matter to be proved during trial based on factors that will be discussed below.

Illustrating the Meaning of Official Policy

In *Webster v. City of Houston* (1984:841), the Fifth Circuit said that "a municipality is liable under Section 1983 for a deprivation of rights protected by the Constitution or federal laws that is inflicted pursuant to official policy." It then added that "actions of officers or employees of a municipality do not render the municipality liable under Section 1983 unless they execute official policy as above defined." A few cases will help illustrate this principle.

In *Webster* the use by the police of "throw down" guns created municipal liability because it was established during the trial that the practice was of common knowledge among supervisors in the city. One incident, however, does not a "custom" make. In *Webster* (1984: 842) the court said:

> If actions of employees are . . . to prove a custom [such action] must have occurred for so long or so frequently that [they] warrant . . . the attribution to the governing body of knowledge that the objectionable conduct is the expected practice of city employees [so that] the governing body [is charged] with actual or constructive knowledge of such actions of subordinates.

In a different case also involving the City of Houston, however, the Fifth Circuit Court of Appeals held that there was not sufficient evidence of a widespread custom to impose liability (*Hamilton v. Rodgers*, 1986). In that case, the City of Houston was sued in connection with the alleged racial harassment of the plaintiff, an employee of the Houston Fire Department. The court found that plaintiff's co-workers created an atmosphere of racist bigotry and that plaintiffs supervisors contributed to that environment. There was not enough evidence, however, to establish that high-ranking officers either knew or constructively knew of the persistent racial problem, hence the agency could not be held liable.

In *Fiacco v. City of Rensselaer* (1986), the Second Circuit Court of Appeals affirmed a jury verdict against a city whose police officers used excessive force in arresting the plaintiff. In that case, the court found that the city was "knowingly and deliberately indifferent to the possibility that its police officers were wont to use excessive force and that this indifference was demonstrated by the failure of the City defendants to exercise reasonable care in investigating claims of police brutality in order to supervise the officers in the proper use of force" (1986:326). Evidence was introduced during the trial that the policy of nonsupervision of police officers amounted to deliberate indifference to their use force. Such evidence included proof of the city's failure to adopt measures to deal with complaints of police brutality and of its failure to reasonably investigate such complaints. The policy implications of the *Fiacco* case for police departments are clear—each department must have a policy of active supervision of subordinates and prompt investigation of complaints of police brutality.

In another case, the First Circuit Court of Appeals upheld a jury verdict against a city for its failure to train its police department adequately, leading to the use of excessive force against the plaintiff by two police officers (*Wierstak v. Heffernan*, 1986:975). The court said:

> There was evidence that the City of Worcester failed to properly train its officers about policies on the use of firearms, high-speed chases, and road blocks. There was evidence that the City failed to instruct its officers on the amount of force that should be used in making an arrest and on the need to inspect injured prisoners as required [by state law] . . .. The testimony further showed that the City never conducted any sort of investigation into the circumstances of the plaintiff's arrest nor his claims of brutality . . .

The *Wierstak* decision points to the importance of proper training and investigation of complaints about the conduct of the police. Inaction in either of these areas may lead to agency liability.

In *Harris v. City of Pagedale* (1987), the Eighth Circuit Court of Appeals imposed liability on a city, based on custom. In *Harris*, an arrestee who had been sexually assaulted by a police officer brought a civil rights action against the city and the officer. The plaintiff proved that the city failed to take any remedial action with regard to physical and sexual abuse by police officers, and that such failure amounted to deliberate indifference rather than mere negligence. Plaintiff presented evidence of a number of incidents of sexual misconduct by various officers, particularly the officer who arrested the plaintiff, and that city officials in positions of authority had repeatedly been notified of the offensive acts, but did nothing. The court held that: (1) plaintiff established that there existed in the city a custom of failing to investigate or act on citizen complaints of physical and sexual misconduct by officers; (2) evidence supported the determination that the board of aldermen, its members, and the chief of police had final authority to establish the custom of deliberate indifference to a known pattern of misconduct; and (3) plaintiff established that the custom proximately caused the sexual assault. The City of Pagedale was held liable.

The aforementioned cases, as well as others, show that two elements are necessary for the imposition of liability upon a municipality or agency for the actions of lower-ranking employees. First, it must be established that the alleged violation resulted from an "official policy" or custom. Second, it must be proven that the policy or custom was attributable to the municipality through the policymaker. Factors indicating that the policymaker had actual or constructive knowledge of a custom may include:

1. the presence of supervisory personnel at the scene of the violation:

2. the extent to which the policymaker oversees operational aspects of the organization;

3. the incident review process used by the policymaker; and

4. the method used to gain control and compliance of employees.

Factors indicating that the action of a lower-ranking employee was based on a custom attributable to the municipality may include:

1. the frequency of the violations;

2. the extent to which the practice was routinized by employees;

3. the extent to which the practice was accepted by supervisors;

4. the extent to which the action represented shared beliefs of employees;

5. the number and unanimity of employees involved in the violation:

6. retention, failure to discipline, or failure to investigate the violating employee; and

7. the policymaker's failure to prevent future violations (*Bordanaro v. McLeod*, 1989).

While these factors are indicative of the existence of an official policy or custom, courts view custom in the "totality of the circumstances" surrounding the violation. The presence or absence of a single factor usually does not determine liability. For example, in one case, although it was shown that a police department had six incidents of police brutality within a single precinct, the court concluded that the length of time encompassed by the incidents (ten years) and the number of officers employed by the department (over 10,000) precluded a finding that these violations showed a pattern or custom indicating tolerance for police brutality (*Ramos v. City of Chicago*, 1989). Here, the court could not say that the six incidents in and of themselves were evidence of a widespread behavior or a generally accepted practice by police employees.

The term "official policy" has been given various meanings by different courts and the definition used above by the Fifth Circuit is not necessarily the definition used by all courts. Any definition, though, will inevitably include some of the characteristics used in the Fifth Circuit definition—including the concept of a policy officially promulgated by decisionmakers and the concept of custom. Unless the United States Supreme Court settles the issue, the meaning of "official policy" and "custom" will continue to be tentative and changing, varying from one court to another.

Official Policymakers

The crucial question for municipal liability (as distinguished from the liability of an individual police officer) for the acts of employees is: Who is an official policymaker? The answer: the final policymaking authority, as determined by state law. Not every city employee, or even the majority of city employees, comes under this category. The issue was decided, although not clearly, by the Supreme Court in *City of St. Louis v. Praprotnik* (1988). In that case, a management-level employee (an architect) in one of the city agencies in St. Louis successfully appealed a temporary suspension by his supervisor to the Civil Service Commission. Two years later, however, the employee was transferred to a clerical position in another city agency. The following year, he was laid off by the supervisor. The employee sued, claiming that his dismissal was in retaliation for his successful appeal and that the layoff was in violation of his First Amendment right and the right to due process.

The jury found the City of St. Louis liable. The Court of Appeals affirmed the jury's verdict, saying that the employee's layoff was brought about by an unconstitutional city policy. Applying a test under which a "policymaker" was determined to be one whose employment decisions are final in the sense that they are not subjected to *de novo* review by higher-ranking officials, the Court of Appeals then concluded that the City of St. Louis could be held liable for adverse personnel decisions made by the supervisor who laid off the employee.

On appeal, the United States Supreme Court reversed the decision. In a 7-1 vote, the Court threw out a $15,000 award against the City of St. Louis, saying that generally only the highest ranking city officials can commit constitutional violations that make the city liable. In the case of St. Louis, that is limited to the mayor, the aldermen, and the civil service commission. Said the Court:

> The identification of officials having "final policymaking authority" is a question of state (including local) law, rather than a question of fact for the jury. Here, it appears that petitioners City Charter gives the authority to set employment policy to the mayor and aldermen, who are empowered to enact ordinances, and to the Commission, whose function is to hear employees' appeals. Petitioner (the City of St. Louis) cannot be held liable unless respondent proved the existence of an unconstitutional policy promulgated by officials having such authority (4205).

The Court then added that the mayor and aldermen did not enact an ordinance permitting retaliatory transfers or layoffs. Nor had the Commission indicated that such actions were permissible. The layoff was a decision made by the agency supervisor who, under state law, was not an "official policymaker." Such action therefore did not constitute official policy for which the City of St. Louis could be held liable. The supervisor, but not the agency, could be held liable for the act.

The *Praprotnik* case is important because the decision makes it difficult for plaintiffs to win lawsuits against a city government based on allegations that low-ranking officials violated their rights. Moreover, it says that a city cannot be sued successfully based on claims that high-ranking officials failed to override a subordinate's decision that violated an employee's rights. Instead, it must be established that the violation was the result of official policy and custom rather than a mere failure to override a subordinate's decision. The case also says that the determination of which officials have final policymaking authority is a question of state and local law, rather than a question of fact for the jury to decide.

On the county level, the sheriff is the law enforcement arm of the government, usually under state law, and therefore a sheriff is considered an official policymaker. A policy of inadequate training of deputies or ratification of unconstitutional conduct by the sheriff is attributable to the county, hence liability attaches (*Marchese v. Lucas*, 1985). On the other hand, a constable is not a policymaking official of a county, since he has no control over his selection, training, or performance of duty. Unlike a judge or sheriff, a constable has no choice of objectives and means, hence what a constable does or promulgates cannot be construed as official policy (*Rhode v. Denson*, 1985). Police chiefs, however, have been found to be policymakers and a policy or custom promoted by the chief can lead to municipality liability.

The Good Faith Defense and Agency Defendants

In the past, agency defendants have argued that even though their policies may have been unconstitutional, they should be afforded the defense of "good faith." In *Owen v. City of Independence* (1980), however, the Court said that a municipality sued under Section 1983 cannot invoke the good faith defense, which is available to its officers and employees, if its policies are violative of constitutional rights. In that case, a police chief was dismissed by the City Manager and City Council for certain misdeeds while in office. The police chief was not given any type of hearing or due process rights because the city charter under which the City Manager and City Council acted did not give him any rights prior to dismissal. The Court held that the City Manager and members of the City Council acted in good faith because they were authorized by the provisions of the City Charter, but that the city itself could not invoke the good faith defense, hence the city could be liable. The rationale for this decision is that the plaintiff has suffered injury and such injury is compensable. It is unfair to impose liability on the officers who were merely carrying out agency policy. The agency that drafted the policy and promulgated it must therefore bear the responsibility for the injury and the financial loss. Said the Court in the *Owen* case:

> The innocent individual who is harmed by an abuse of governmental authority is assured that he will be compensated for his injury. The offending official, so long as he conducts himself in good faith, may go about his business secure in the knowledge that a qualified immunity will protect him from personal liability for damages that are more appropriately chargeable to the populace as a whole. And the public will be forced to bear only the costs of injury inflicted by the execution of a government's policy or custom, whether made by its lawmakers or by those whose edicts or acts may fairly be said to represent official policy (657).

Single Acts and Agency Liability

Will local governments be held liable under Section 1983 for failure to train or supervise based on the single act of misconduct of a police officer? The answer is no, but with an important exception. In *Oklahoma City v. Tuttle* (1985), action was brought for the fatal shooting by a police officer of a suspect who had no weapon and did not threaten the officer. Survivors of the suspect sued the officer and the city, alleging negligent failure to train and negligent supervision. There was sufficient evidence during trial to support a finding of an official policy or custom of gross negligence, but such finding was based mainly on the single incident in question. Was this single incident sufficient to hold the agency liable? The Court gave a qualified answer: "Proof of a single incident of unconstitutional activity is not sufficient to impose liability . . . . unless it was caused by an existing unconstitutional municipal policy, which policy can be attributed to a municipal policymaker" (814). Similar results were achieved in *Rodriguez v. Avita* (1989), where a single shooting incident constituted a violation of constitutional rights but failed to be sufficient proof of "official" policy or custom of the agency.

This principle is significant because it rejects liability based on a single incident, but allows an important exception—if the incident was caused by an existing, unconstitutional municipal policy, and the policy can be attributed to a municipal policymaker. That exception was used earlier by the Court to impose liability in the case of *Pembaur v. City of Cincinnati* (1986). In *Pembaur* the county prosecutor made official policy, and thereby exposed his municipal employer to liability, by instructing law enforcement officers to make a forcible entry, without search warrant, of an office in order to serve capiases (a form of warrant issued by the judge) on persons thought to be there. The officers were trying to arrest two employees in a doctor's office who had failed to appear before a grand jury. The Court decided that this violated the Fourth Amendment rights of the office owners and concluded that the City of Cincinnati could be held liable because the decision by, a county prosecutor and the sheriff's forced entry, even on a single occasion, constituted official policy or custom.

To summarize: a single act generally creates no municipal liability. What is needed is a persistent pattern of conduct that constitutes a custom. A single act may, however, create municipal liability if the act was caused by an existing unconstitutional "official" policy that can be attributed to a municipal policymaker. Moreover, a single act that violates plaintiffs constitutional rights may also be the basis for individual officer liability.

Agency Liability for Failure to Train Police Officers

Official policies that become the subject of lawsuits under 42 U.S.C. § 1983 may be the product either of affirmative acts by the agency or the failure of the agency to act. The allegation of inadequate or improper training of police officers is frequently the basis of a "failure to act" claim. This issue, after years of uncertainty, was finally resolved by the United States Supreme Court in *City of Canton v.*

Harris (1989). The Court said that failure to train can be the basis of liability under Section 1983 for cities or municipalities if such failure to train amounts to "deliberate indifference."

In the *Harris* case, plaintiff Geraldine Harris was arrested and brought to the police station in a police wagon. Upon arrival at the station, Harris was found sitting on the floor of the wagon. When asked if she needed medical attention, Harris responded with an incoherent remark. While being processed, Harris slumped to the floor twice. Eventually, she was released and taken by an ambulance, provided by her family, to a nearby hospital where she was diagnosed as suffering from several emotional ailments. She was hospitalized for one week, and later received outpatient treatment for one year. Harris brought a 1983 suit against the city and its officials, claiming that they violated her constitutional right to due process.

Evidence was presented during the trial which indicated that, pursuant to a city regulation, shift commanders in the Canton Police Department were authorized to determine, in their sole discretion, whether a detainee required medical care. Testimony was also presented stating that the shift commanders were not provided with any special training (beyond first-aid training) to make a determination as to when to ask for medical care for an injured detainee. The District Court decided for Harris on the medical claim; the Sixth Circuit Court of Appeals affirmed that decision. The case was appealed to the United States Supreme Court.

The Court held that failure to train can be the basis of liability under Section 1983. In an unanimous decision, the Court held that cities and municipalities may be held liable for damages if the failure to train is based on "deliberate indifference" to the rights of those with whom the police come into contact. While the nine justices agreed that "deliberate indifference" should be the standard for liability, it did not define with precision (probably because this term defies precise definition) what "deliberate indifference" means. The Court came closest to defining that term when it stated that, "it may happen that in light of the duties assigned to specific officers or employees the need for more or different training is so obvious, and the inadequacy so likely to result in violation of constitutional rights, that the policymakers of the city can reasonably be said to have been deliberately indifferent to the need" (1205).

The Court then set forth what may be considered additional requisites for liability based on "deliberate indifference." These are:

1. the focus must be on the adequacy of the training program in relation to the tasks the particular officer must perform;

2. the fact that a particular officer may be unsatisfactorily trained will not alone result in city liability because the officer's shortcoming may have resulted from factors other than a faulty training program;

3. it is not sufficient to impose liability if it can be proved that an injury or accident could have been avoided if an officer had better or more training; and

4. the identified deficiency in a city's training program must be closely related to the ultimate injury.

The *Harris* case brings good news and bad news to potential plaintiffs. The good news is that for the first time the United States Supreme Court has ruled that cities and municipalities may be liable for inadequate training of police officers. The bad news is that most plaintiffs will find it difficult to meet the tough legal standard of "deliberate indifference" set out by the Court as the criterion for liability.

In *Harris*, the City of Canton argued that a municipality can be found liable under § 1983 only if the policy in question is itself unconstitutional. Had that argument prevailed, the City would not have been liable because the Court itself admitted that "there can be little doubt that on its face the city's policy regarding medical treatment for detainees is constitutional." The Court, however, rejected this argument, holding instead that a city may be liable even if the city's policy is constitutional, if the lack of training amounts to deliberate indifference. The basis for liability in *Harris* was not the policy itself but the lack of implementation of that policy.

It is also important to note that in *Harris* (1989:1206), the Court concluded that the "evidence in the record does not meet the standard of Section 1983," and therefore remanded the case to the trial court to afford Harris an opportunity to prove her case under the "deliberate indifference" standard set by the Court.

Using the *Harris* case as precedent, the United States First Circuit Court of Appeals decided *Bordanaro v. McLeod* (1989). The facts of that case are that in the summer of 1982 an off-duty police officer and a female were at a motel bar. Shortly after their arrival, an altercation began between the officer and two other patrons. The officer was badly beaten in the fight and ejected from the bar. He then called the police department to report the incident; the entire night-watch of the department was dispatched to the scene. Upon arrival at the bar the officers found the glass front door locked; they demanded admittance. When the manager hesitated, they shattered the door and threatened to kill the occupants of the lounge. Those involved in the earlier altercation had fled to a room within the motel and the officers pursued them, brandishing "nightsticks, clubs, bats, tire-irons and an axe in addition to their service revolvers" (1153). Instead of accepting the manager's offer to open the door with a pass key, officers drilled a hole and sprayed mace into the room while firing shots into the door. After the officers forcibly entered the room, the plaintiffs were beaten unconscious, and one died from the injuries.

A civil rights action was brought under 42 U.S.C. §§ 1983 against the municipality, mayor, police chief and several individual officers claiming that the police action constituted numerous constitutional violations. On appeal, the First Circuit discussed in detail the issue of municipality liability for police misconduct. The court reviewed the trial evidence and affirmed the jury's finding of municipal liability for failure to train as well as the imposition of punitive damages against the chief of police and the mayor. Liability was based on the following findings:

1. the department was operating under rules and regulations developed and distributed to the officers in the 1960s;

2. the department's rules and regulations failed to address modern issues in law enforcement;

3. the department failed to provide officers with training beyond that received in the police academy;

4. the City actively discouraged officers from seeking training;

5. there was no supervisory training;

6. the chief of police haphazardly meted out discipline and failed to discipline the officers in the current incident until after they were indicted; and

7. there was no internal investigation of the incident until one year after its occurrence.

The court found liability for failure to train based on the "deliberate indifference standard" as well as liability for the promotion of an "official" policy based on a custom of unconstitutional use of force and unlawful search and seizure. The *Bordanaro* case applies the standards set forth by the United States Supreme Court in *Harris* to a specific set of facts and concludes that there was deliberate indifference. The *Harris* standards for municipal liability in negligent failure to train cases tend to be conceptual and subjective, but they can be applied with a degree of certainty to specific cases.

Conclusion

It is clear that municipalities and police agencies may now be held liable, if what police officers do is traceable to an official policy. The term "official policy" eludes precise definition, and its specifics may vary from court to court. Generally, however, it refers to a written policy statement, ordinance, regulation, or decision that is officially adopted and promulgated by the municipality, and a persistent, widespread practice of city officials or employees which, although not authorized by officially adopted and promulgated policy, is so common and well-settled as to constitute a custom that fairly represents municipal policy. This single "official policy" standard for liability does away with prior decisions that based liability on the degree of negligence rather than on agency complicity.

The determination of who is an official policymaker whose actions might lead to municipal liability is governed by state law. Decisions made by officials who, under state law, are not policymakers do not lead to municipal liability, hence not every agency policy leads to liability. Actions of lower-level administrative officials do not lead to agency liability. There remains, however, the question of who is an official policymaker under state law. That answer will vary from state to state depending upon statute or case law.

Cities or municipalities can be sued for negligent failure to train, if such failure amounts to deliberate indifference. Guidelines for determining deliberate indifference have been set, but they are so broad as to be almost subjective. Nonetheless, they can be applied to specific cases—as one Circuit Court of Appeals has done.

Judicial progress has been made in this complex and important area of law. It should be clear to plaintiffs that the "deep pockets" approach will not succeed every time a police officer inflicts injury on a member of the public. The "official policy" doctrine sets the standard by which municipal liability is determined. This doctrine has serious implications for municipal agencies, but at the same time it indicates how municipal liability can be avoided. Written departmental policies are a necessity, but more than that, the policies must be reviewed carefully to ensure that they comport with statutes and the Constitution. Persistent policies and practices in the department that may not be written but may come under the category of "custom" must also be carefully monitored to make sure they are legal and constitutional. This requires constant policy review and ongoing supervision, particularly in view of the possibility that liability may be imposed not only because the agency policymakers knew, but also that they "should have known" about the existence of unconstitutional policies and practices. While these requirements may pose difficulty for some municipalities, in the long run they can only lead to more professional police departments.

Note

[1] Although states are immune from liability under Section 1983, that protection has largely been waived in state tort cases—either by statute or court decisions. Generally, states and state agencies may be sued under state tort law for what their officers do. Such waiver is usually found in state tort acts, the specifics of which vary from state to state. The federal government has a Federal Tort Claims Act that waives immunity in many cases involving federal employees (28 U.S.C. § 1348).

Cases

Bennett v. City of Slidell, 735 F.2d 861 (5th Cir. 1984).
Bordanaro v. McLeod, 871 F.2d 1151 (1st Cir. 1989).
City of Canton v. Harris, 109 S. Ct. 1197 (1989).
City of St. Louis v. Praprotnik, 108 S. Ct. 915 (1988).
Fiacco v. City of Rensselaer, 783 F.2nd 319 (2nd Cir. 1986).
Grandstaff v. City of Borger, 767 F.2d 161 (5th Cir. 1985).
Hamilton v. Rodgers, 791 F.2d 439 (5th Cir. 1986).
Harris v. City of Pagedale, 821 F.2d 499 (8th Cir. 1987).
Marchese v. Lucas, 758 F.2nd 181 (6th Cir. 1985).
Monell v. Department of Social Services, 436 U.S. 658 (1978).
Oklahoma City v. Tuttle, 471 U.S. 808 (1985).
Owen v. City of Independence, 445 U.S. 622 (1980).
Pembaur v. City of Cincinnati, 475 U.S. 469 (1986).
Ramos v. City of Chicago, 707 F. Supp. 345 (N.D. Ill. 1989).
Rhode v. Denson, 776 F.2d 107 (5th Cir. 1985).
Rodriguez v. Avita, 871 F.2d 552 (5th Cir. 1989).
Webster v. City of Houston, 735 F.2d 838 (5th Cir. 1984).
Wierstak v. Heffernan, 789 F.2d 968 (1st Cir. 1986).
Will v. Michigan Department of State Police, 45 C.L.R. 3087 (1989).

Forces of Change in Police Policy: The Impact of *Tennessee v. Garner*

Samuel Walker
University of Nebraska at Omaha

Lorie Fridell
Florida State University

In 1985, the U.S. Supreme Court handed down the decision in *Tennessee v. Garner* (471 U.S. 1), which restricts the circumstances under which law enforcement officers may use deadly force to arrest. Following the announcement of this decision, newspapers and news magazines proclaimed that the Supreme Court had struck down approximately 21 state statutes—implying that this decision would have a major impact on deadly force policy nationwide. Though the information regarding the statutes was true, the implication that this decision would force major changes in law enforcement policy was not.

This article explores the change process relative to deadly force law and policy, culminating in the U.S. Supreme Court decision on this topic. We include data from a survey of police departments in major U.S. cities regarding the impact of *Tennessee v. Garner* on their policies. The survey results and the historical analysis of the change process are discussed in terms of future developments in police policy and the role of the U.S. Supreme Court in those developments.

The Garner Decision

The *Garner* case involved the death, at the hands of police, of a fifteen-year-old male who had broken into an unoccupied house and stolen a ring and a coin purse containing ten dollars. Memphis police were on the scene as a result of a neighbor's call and Officer Hymon, in the backyard, saw Garner running towards a six-foot high chain-link fence. Aided with a flashlight, the officer was able to view the suspect's hands and, resultingly, was "reasonably sure" that Garner was unarmed. He yelled for the suspect to stop, but Garner started over the fence. The officer believed that the suspect would successfully escape if allowed to continue over the fence. Thus, consistent with the Tennessee statute and Memphis Police Department policy, Officer Hymon fired at Garner, hitting him in the back of the head and killing him.

Garner's father brought a 42 U.S.C. Section 1983 action in Federal District Court claiming violation of his son's Fourth, Fifth, Sixth, Eighth, and Fourteenth Amendment rights. The District Court found the Tennessee deadly force statute constitutional. This common law any-fleeing-felon statute allowed officers to use deadly force to arrest if it was necessary to capture or overcome the resistance of a felon. On appeal the Sixth Circuit Court of Appeals found the Tennessee statute in violation of Fourth Amendment protections against unreasonable seizures insofar as it allowed for use of deadly force against nondangerous, as well as dangerous, fleeing felons (*Garner v. Memphis P.D.*, 710 F.2d 240).

The State of Tennessee appealed to the U.S. Supreme Court which granted certiorari and held 6-3 that, with regard to the apprehension of fleeing felons:

> [deadly force] may not be used unless it is necessary to prevent the escape and the officer has probable cause to believe that the suspect poses a significant threat of death or serious physical injury to the officer or others.

The focus was again on the "reasonableness" of a deadly force seizure per the Fourth Amendment. The Court opinion, authored by Justice White, focused on the determination of "reasonableness" by "balancing the extent of the intrusion against the need for it." The intrusion—taking of the suspect's life—was considered "unmatched." On the other side were "governmental interests in effective law enforcement." Though it was noted that the law enforcement goals of arresting felons and encouraging the nonviolent surrender thereof were important, the Court was not convinced that the common law any-fleeing-felon statute was an effective means to accomplish these goals, at least not effective enough to "justify the killing of non-violent suspects."

The Court reviewed "prevailing rules in individual jurisdictions" to determine whether the common law rule was "an essential attribute of the arrest power in all felony cases" and, relatedly, whether omitting that policy option would "hamper effective law enforcement." It found a "long-term movement . . . away from the rule that deadly force may be used against any fleeing felon" and that fewer than half the states retained a common law any-fleeing-felon statute.

An alternative assessment of "prevailing rules" is of police department policies, for many are more restrictive than the state statute. The Court cited two relevant studies. A 1974 study found that the police departments in most large U.S. cities limited use of deadly force to dangerous fleeing felons (Boston Police Department, 1974). An International Association of Chiefs of Police (IACP) Survey found that, as of 1980, 86.8 percent of the police departments in cities with populations greater than 250,000 had policies more restrictive than the common law any fleeing felon rule (Matulia, 1982). The Court noted that ". . . a majority of police departments in this country have forbidden the use of deadly force against nonviolent suspects" (*Tennessee v. Garner,* 11).

Relying in large part on the assessment of current state laws and departmental policies, the Court determined that "shooting nondangerous fleeing suspects is (not) so vital as to outweigh the suspect's interest in his own life." And, as such, the Court ruled the common law any-fleeing-felon statute unconstitutional.

Deadly Force Law and Policy

Sources of control over use of deadly force are statutory law, case law, and police department policy. Three basic models reflect virtually all U.S. guidelines in this area: the common law any-fleeing-felon policy, the forcible felony laws, and the Model Penal Code. As noted above, Tennessee statutes and the Memphis Police Department policy reflected the common law any-fleeing-felon rule which allows an officer to use deadly force if it is necessary to capture or overcome the resistance of any felon. At common law all felonies were punishable by death, thus the use of lethal force to effectuate arrest was seen as merely expediting execution. This is the broadest of the three policy types and, as noted below, had been the subject of numerous court challenges even prior to *Garner.*

Unlike the common law rule that allowed deadly force against any fleeing felon, the "forcible felony" laws restrict deadly force to persons suspected of certain specified felonies that pose a risk of great bodily harm or death.

The American Law Institute model penal code (Section 3.08), proposed in 1962, limits deadly force to felony arrests where the officer believes:

1. the crime for which the arrest is made involved conduct, including the use or threatened use of deadly force; or

2. there is a substantial risk that the person to be arrested will cause death or serious bodily harm if his apprehension is delayed.

This latter model most closely resembles the U.S. Supreme Court rule presented in *Garner.*

Challenges to the common law any-fleeing-felon rule—the least restrictive model—date back to the late nineteenth century. The bulk of the cases focused on violations of the cruel and unusual punishment clause of the Eighth Amendment (*Cunningham v. Ellington* and *Wiley v. Memphis P.D.*), the seizure restrictions of the Fourth Amendment (*Landrum v. Moats*), and the equal protection and due process clauses of the Fourteenth Amendment (*Cunningham* and *Mattis v. Schnarr*).

The federal circuit courts have been divided in their rulings. The Second Circuit Court ruled on the constitutionality of the Connecticut common law rule in the context of a 42 U.S.C. Section 1983 action for deprivation of a fleeing felon's life without due process of law. The court held the statute constitutional noting that, though there was a trend toward more restrictive deadly force law, this trend was "... not so momentous or compelling as to require us to recognize a Section 1983 action to lie in the situation of this case" (*Jones v. Marshall*).

In *Mattis v. Schnarr*, the Eighth Circuit Court held the Missouri common law statute unconstitutional because it violated due process rights of the Fifth and Fourteenth Amendments. The U.S. Supreme Court, however, vacated the decision, maintaining that "no live case or controversy" was presented (*Ashcroft v. Mattis*). Soon after the Eighth Circuit Court decision, the Sixth Circuit upheld the constitutionality of the common law statute of Tennessee in *Wiley v. Memphis P.D.* Just six years later, this same court ruled in *Garner v. Memphis P.D.* that the Tennessee code was unconstitutional.

The Impact of *Garner*: A Survey of Policies

As noted above, the announcement in the media of *Tennessee v. Garner* left the impression that major changes in police policy and practice were forthcoming as a result of the U.S. Supreme Court's decision. Fyfe and Walker (1990) examined the effect of *Garner* on case law and statutory law; the current study focuses on the effect of this case on departmental policy.

To assess the effect of *Garner* on police department policy, surveys were sent to the police departments in the 100 most populated cities in the U.S. which asked each Chief of police whether—as a result of the *Garner* decision—the department had to modify its use of force policy. Although there is some reason to believe that *Garner* probably affected small police agencies more than large police agencies (Blumberg, 1989), we chose to survey the 100 largest cities (ranging in population size from 160,000 to 7,165,000) because these areas account for the vast majority of deadly force incidents and thus provide the most relevant target group for assessing the impact of the decision on actual police practice. The surveys were sent out in January of 1988. Ninety-six police departments responded.[1]

The cities and their responses are contained in Table 1. Sixty-seven of the cities (69.8%) did not have to revise their deadly force policies following *Garner*.

They had previously adopted policies in accordance with, or more restrictive than, the Supreme Court rule. The remaining 29 police departments (30.2%)—listed in Table 2—reported that the Garner decision necessitated a revision of policy.

There is no discernible variation by geographical area. Thirty-three percent (9 of 27) of the cities in the West had to modify their policies, and 29 percent (11 of 38), 26 percent (5 of 19), and 33 percent (4 of 12) of the cities in the South, Midwest, and Northeast, respectively, had to modify their policies. Neither is there any relationship between city size and need to revise policy for the cities included in the sample.

Based on previous surveys, we would expect that only a small number of the 29 cities that modified their policies had the common law rule in effect at the time of the *Garner* decision. The IACP survey reported that in 1980 only four of 50 police departments in cities with populations over 250,000 had policies that permitted the shooting of any fleeing felons. A 1982 survey reported in the *Garner amicus* brief of the Police Foundation found that only one of 75 police departments within cities of 100,000 or more retained a common law policy. Thus, it is reasonable to assume that most of the revisions that occurred were not major revisions—for instance, moving from a forcible felony to a dangerous felony policy to accommodate the holding in *Garner.*

The Court, Police Policy, and the Process of Change

The data presented here come as no great surprise to anyone familiar with the recent literature on police firearms policy. As the *Garner* briefs argued, most big city police departments had moved in the direction of more restrictive shooting policies (Geller, 1982) and the Court cited this evidence in its decision. Indeed, the extent to which most police departments had abandoned the fleeing felon standard accounts for the virtual absence of vocal protest from the police about the Court's ruling.

The most significant aspects of *Garner* and its impact, then, lies in the larger context of police policy making. We find here a process that is the reverse of what we generally expect with regard to the Court and police procedures. Instead of being in the advance guard of change—enunciating new standards of Constitutional law and forcing the police to conform to them—the Court trailed far behind police departments in developing standards to protect individual rights. For this issue, the Court was serving not as an agent of social change, but rather, as the force to bring into compliance law enforcement agencies that were not conforming to existing law enforcement norms.

Models of the Change Process

The literature on police firearms policy clearly indicates that significant changes in policy occurred prior to the *Garner* decision. A number of different forces—both internal and external—were at work to produce these changes, including statutory change, voluntary actions by police administrators, political pressure by civil rights and community groups, the "due process revolution," and case law expanding the liability of departments for the actions of their officers (Sherman, 1978; Geller, 1982).

In an attempt to model the change process, we outline briefly the principal forces for change, with reference to police firearms policy.

The Classic Professional Model

The classic professional model involves a process of self-governance. In theory at least, professions govern their own affairs through associations that promulgate standards of professional conduct (Moore, 1970). There has been considerable debate over whether policing qualifies as a true profession. We do not plan to engage that debate here, since most of it concerns on-the-street police work. From an organizational perspective, policing has some of the key attributes of a profession: national professional associations promulgating minimum standards.

With respect to firearms policy, restrictive policies were often adopted at the initiative of a reform-oriented chief executive—the 1972 New York City policy being the most notable example (Fyfe, 1979). Uelmen's (1973) early study of firearms policy concluded that the personality of the chief executive was the most important factor explaining the enormous variations he found.

Few if any observers of the subject of police use of deadly force, however, seriously believe that police executives in the pre-*Garner* years adopted restrictive shooting policies wholly on their own initiative. Rather, it would appear that they were prompted in large part because of the continuing protests about police shootings by civil rights and community groups, or what Sherman (1978) calls "community outrage."

The classic professional model might also include the Model Penal Code standard for police firearms policy as an example of change resulting from the work of a professional association. The Model Penal Code, first promulgated in 1962, did not emerge from the law enforcement community, however. It was a project of the elite of the legal profession, specifically the American Law Institute, and thus, is more properly viewed as an externally initiated reform. But even associations more closely aligned with the police profession (e.g., International Association of Chiefs of Police) do not have the power to force agency conformity to the standards they set forth. Thus, the reliance is still on other forces of change, and the result is that a number of departments will lag behind the norms until a Court decision, such as *Garner,* mandates compliance.

Statutory Change

Police reform through statutory change has particular relevance for this subject, since deadly force is one of the few areas of police behavior governed by state statute. Change in this area has primarily involved the adoption of the Model Penal Code standard. This process did not begin until 1971 but then proceeded rapidly. Sherman reported in 1978 that seven states had adopted the Model Penal Code language, while ten others had statutes with language more restrictive than the old common law standard. By the time of *Garner* more than one-half of the states had moved away from the permissive common law standard, with two adopting the Model Penal Code standard verbatim and another eighteen enacting policies with restrictive language.

We cannot attribute these changes to any special concern with police use of deadly force, however. Adoption of the Model Penal Code was usually the result of a general recodification of the criminal law. As Fyfe and Walker (1990) note, legislators have little to gain from introducing or supporting legislation that appears to reduce police power.

Change Through Political Pressure

Political activity by civil rights and community groups is another important source of change in policing and may provide legislative or administrative reform. In 1978 Sherman observed that "community outrage" was "a more direct source of pressure" than statutory revisions in "effecting change in police department administrative policies . . ." The adoption of a restrictive shooting policy by the New York City Police Department in 1972, for example, was probably the result of Police Commissioner Patrick V. Murphy's sensitivity to police-community relations.

There can be little doubt that conflict between the police and racial minorities has been one of the most important aspects of American policing since the early 1960s and that complaints about discriminatory patterns in police shootings has been a major point of controversy. These protests established the context for change through administrative initiative. In a broader historical perspective, we can argue that police professionalization has always been spurred by external political events. The professionalization movement originated early in this century as part of a broader urban reform movement. Many of its leaders came from outside the law enforcement community (Walker, 1977). The President's Crime Commission of the 1960s, which spurred a massive wave of police reform (one that has not yet played itself out) was prompted by political considerations external to the criminal justice community (Walker, 1980). The Model Penal Code standard on deadly force, for example, was, as noted above, the product of an elite within the legal profession, with little input from the law enforcement community itself (Wechsler, 1952). In short, it too can be seen as an element of change arising from outside the law enforcement community.

Court-Initiated Change

The Supreme Court became one of the most important forces for change in the entire American criminal justice system in the 1960s. A series of landmark decisions, collectively referred to as the "due process revolution," effected significant changes in all aspects of the criminal justice process.

Some commentators argue that the important Court decisions regarding the police, beginning with *Mapp* in 1961, stimulated wide-ranging reforms. These included higher recruitment standards, improved training, better management and supervision of personnel. In some respects, the Court stimulated reform efforts that have acquired lives of their own. The accreditation movement in both law enforcement and corrections, for example, began in large part as a move to avoid litigation (CALEA, 1988). The growth of administrative rulemaking—the development of specific written procedures and the codification of those procedures in policy manuals—was greatly stimulated by Court scrutiny of police behavior (McGowan, 1972; Davis, 1975).

There is some evidence that lower federal court rulings forced some police departments to change their deadly force policies. A 1978 decision by the Eighth Circuit Court of Appeals invalidated the Omaha Police Department policy which followed the common law standard (*Landrum v. Moats*).

Change in Laws Regarding Civil Liability

The expansion of civil liability of police departments by the courts gave impetus to much of the litigation mentioned above which led to changes in departmental policies. The *Garner* case itself would not have been decided on the force issue, but for a decision expanding civil liability that was decided while *Garner* was being processed through the court system. According to Fyfe and Walker (1990), "absent *Monell* [described below], all the defendants in *Garner* would have escaped liability, and the case would have resulted in no change in the constitutional status of the any fleeing felon rule."

In *Monell v. Department of Social Services of the City of New York*, the U.S. Supreme Court held that units of local government may be liable for the unconstitutional actions of officers that stem from "official policy." Thus, a citizen could sue local governmental entities for a violation of his or her civil rights if the government worker who violated those rights was acting in accordance with "a policy statement, ordinance, regulation, or decision officially adopted and promulgated by municipal officers" or in accordance with "custom." This decision led to departmental review of and revision of policies and practices. Although it has not been specifically documented, it seems highly likely that the *Monell* decision was an important factor in the adoption of restrictive policies by departments, both in anticipation of and in response to lawsuits.

Summary: A Complex Model of the Change Process

In summary, we can posit the following model of the change process in policing: changes in police policy do not result from any single factor; many forces are at work simultaneously and they interact with each other in a dynamic and complex fashion (Walker, 1986). Thus, administrative changes are often the result of political pressure and/or litigation. Litigation itself is frequently viewed as a political strategy by civil rights groups (Littlejohn, 1981) and becomes more attractive and effective as more "deep pockets" become liable. Litigation may set in motion reform efforts that have broader effects—as in the accreditation movement. Pressure brought by political activity creates a constituency for adoption of standards independently recommended by professional associations—as in the case of the Model Penal Code. Successful litigation often forces administrative and/or statutory change.

The Court, The Police, and the Future of Individual Rights

Our analysis of the change process in policing has important implications for the protection of individual rights in an era when the Supreme Court not only appears disinclined to do so in the criminal justice field but seems eager to weaken existing standards. Because of the great initiatives of the Warren Court—on the police, on other criminal justice agencies, on so many other aspects of American society—many rights advocates came to believe that the Court is the primary, if not the only means of protecting individual rights. Our argument here is that alternate routes to the protection of individual rights are available as viable options.

A very broad consensus exists regarding the trend in police firearms policy sustained by *Garner.* One finds little dissent from the arguments (1) that more restrictive shooting policies represent an appropriate standard of reasonableness; (2) that they have substantially reduced the number of firearms discharges and persons shot and killed; (3) that this overall reduction appears to include a significant reduction in the racial disparity among persons shot and killed (Sherman and

Cohn, 1986); (4) and that these improvements have been achieved at no cost in terms of either increased crime or increased risk to police officers (Fyfe, 1979). In short, one of the most significant rights-oriented reforms was achieved without direct benefit of a Supreme Court ruling.

A similar process of change is occurring in other areas of policing. The most notable involves police handling of domestic violence. Through a similar combination of political pressure, litigation, the development of recommended standards, and administrative rulemaking, many departments have revised their policies. The direction of reform is toward an "arrest-preferred" (and in some instances mandatory arrest) policy, in the interest of providing equal protection of the law to women who are the victims of domestic violence. The verdict is not yet in on whether this approach will achieve its desired goals (Loving, 1980; Sherman and Berk, 1984). Nonetheless, this is another example of a significant "rights-oriented" change that has been taking place at the agency level without specific direction from the U.S. Supreme Court.

Further, in a number of other areas of police work, administrative rulemaking has quietly imposed a network of controls over police discretion, with an eye toward preventing potential abuse of individual rights and/or threats to the lives of citizens (Walker, 1988). A full inventory of these developments is yet to be taken. A review of the Standard Operating Procedure manual of the Omaha Police Division is suggestive of national trends.

The current Omaha SOP manual contains policies with respect to six police actions that reflect the same strategy for controlling police officer behavior that is embodied in current deadly force policy. That strategy involves a written policy confining officer discretion and the requirement of a written report by the officer after each incident. The policies cover all firearms discharges, high speed chases, use of lateral choke holds, use of the baton or mace against a citizen, resisting arrest charges, and arrests on the premises of police headquarters (Omaha Police Division). Each of these is an area fraught with controversy. High speed chases are now recognized as highly dangerous events, to both police officers and citizens (Alpert and Anderson, 1986). The other events are frequently the subject of complaints by racial minorities about the abuse of police authority. None of the policies in question was prompted by a definitive ruling by any federal court. Instead, they have evolved out of a combination of local controversies and an awareness of similar controversies elsewhere in the country.

The available evidence suggests that the process by which most big city police departments revised their deadly forces policies in the pre-*Garner* years was not unique. Rather, it was part of a larger trend toward greater administrative rulemaking in police administration, one that includes increased protections for individual rights. This evidence suggests that, in the face of a conservative Supreme Court, rights advocates have available to them alternative routes to the control of police conduct. These include various combinations of administrative rulemaking, law reform, community-level political activity, and litigation. The true significance of *Garner,* then may be not in what the Court decided but what preceded the decision.

Table 1
Police Departments That Did NOT Have to Revise Their Deadly Force Policies Following *Garner*

67 of 96 cities, or 69.8 percent

West
Albuquerque, NM
Anaheim, CA
Anchorage, AL
Denver, CO
Fresno, CA
Honolulu, HA
Huntington Beach, CA
Long Beach, CA
Los Angeles, CA
Oakland, CA
Portland, OR
Riverside, CA
Sacramento, CA
San Diego, CA
San Francisco, CA
San Jose, CA
Santa Ana, CA
Stockton, CA

Midwest
Akron, OH
Dayton, OH
Des Moines, IA
Fort Wayne, IN
Lincoln, NE
Madison, WI
Milwaukee, WI
Minneapolis, MN
Kansas City, KS
Kansas City, MO
Omaha, NE
St. Paul, MN
Toledo, OH
Wichita, KS

South
Amarillo, TX
Arlington, TX
Atlanta, GA
Austin, TX
Baton Rouge, LA
Birmingham, AL
Charlotte, NC
Columbus, GA
Corpus Christi, TX
Dallas, TX
El Paso, TX
Fort Worth, TX
Houston, TX
Jackson, MS
Knoxville, TN
Lexington-Lafayette, KY
Little Rock, AR
Lubbock, TX
Miami, FL
New Orleans, LA
Raleigh, NC
Richmond, VA
San Antonio, TX
Shreveport, LA
St. Petersburg, FL
Tampa, FL
Tulsa, OK

Northeast
Buffalo, NY
New York, NY
Philadelphia, PA
Pittsburgh, PA
Rochester, NY
Syracuse, NY
Washington, D.C.
Worcester, MA

Table 2
Police Departments That Had to Revise Their Deadly Force Policies Following *Garner*

29 of 96 cities, or 20.2 percent

West	Midwest
Aurora, CO	Chicago, IL
Colorado Springs, CO	Cincinnati, OH
Las Vegas, NV	Columbus, OH
Mesa, AZ	Detroit, MI
Phoenix, AZ	Indianapolis, IN
Salt Lake City, UT	
Seattle, WA	
Spokane, WA	
Tucson, AZ	
South	**Northeast**
Chattanooga, TN	Baltimore, MD
Garland, TX	Boston, MA
Jacksonville, FL	Jersey City, NJ
Louisville, KY	Newark, NJ
Memphis, TN	
Mobile, AL	
Montgomery, AL	
Nashville-Davidson, TN	
Norfolk, VA	
Oklahoma City, OK	
Virginia Beach, VA	

Note

No responses were obtained from the police departments of Cleveland, OH; Grand Rapids, MI; Saint Louis, MO; and Yonkers, NY.

Cases Cited

Ashcroft v. Mattis, 97 S. Ct. 1739, 1977.
Cunningham v. Ellington, 323 F.Supp. 1072, 1971.
Garner v. Memphis Police Department, 710 F.2d 240, 1983.
Jones v. Marshall, 528 F.2d 132, 1975.
Landrum v. Moats, 576 F2d 1320, 1978.
Mattis v. Schnarr, 404 F.Supp. 643, 1975.
Monnell v. Department of Social Services of the City of New York, 436 U.S. 658, 1978.
Tennessee v. Garner, 471 U.S. 1, 1985.
Wiley v. Memphis Police Department, 548 F.2d 1247, 1977.

References

Alpert, G. and P. Anderson (1986). "The Most Deadly Force: Police Pursuits." *Justice Quarterly,* 3:1-14.

Blumberg, M. (1989). "Controlling Police Use of Deadly Force: Assessing Two Decades of Progress," in R. Dunham and G. Alpert (eds.), *Critical Issues in Policing: Contemporary Readings.* Prospect Heights, IL: Waveland Press.

Bohlen, F. and H. Shulman (1927). "Arrest With and Without a Warrant." *University of Pennsylvania,* 75(6):485-504.

Boston Police Department (1974). *The Use of Deadly Force by Boston Police Personnel.* Boston, MA: Planning and Research Division.

Commission on Accreditation for Law Enforcement Agencies (CALEA), (1988). *Standards for Law Enforcement Agencies,* 2nd Edition. Fairfax, VA: Author.

Davis, K. (1975). *Police Discretion.* St. Paul, MN: West Publishing Company.

Fyfe, J. (1979). "Administrative Interventions on Police Shooting Discretion." *Journal of Criminal Justice,* 7:313-335.

Fyfe, J. and J. Walker (1990). "*Garner* Plus Five Years: An Examination of Supreme Court Intervention Into Police Discretion and Legislative Prerogatives." *American Journal of Criminal Justice,* 14(2):167-188.

Geller, W. (1982). "Deadly Force: What We Know." *Journal of Police Science and Administration,* 10(2):168-172.

Littlejohn, E. (1981). "Civil Liability and the Police Officer: The Need for New Deterrents to Police Misconduct." *University of Detroit Journal of Urban Law,* 58:365.

Loving, N. (1980). *Responding to Spouse Abuse and Wife Beating: A Guide for Police.* Washington, D.C.: Police Executive Research Forum.

Matulia, K. (1982). *A Balance of Forces.* Gaithersburg, MD: International Association of Chiefs of Police.

McGowan, C. (1972). "Rulemaking and the Police." *Michigan Law Review,* 70:659.

Moore, W. (1970). *The Professions: Rules and Roles.* New York, NY: Russell Sage.

Moreland, R. (1954). "The Use of Force in Effecting or Resisting Arrest." *Nebraska Law Review,* 33(3):408-426.

Omaha Police Division (n.d.). *Standard Operating Procedures.* Omaha, NE: Author.

Sherman, L. (1978). "Restricting the License to Kill—Recent Developments in Police Use of Deadly Force." *Criminal Law Bulletin,* 14(November):577-583.

Sherman, L. and R. Berk (1984). "The Specific Deterrent Effect of Arrest for Domestic Assault." *American Sociological Review*, 49:261-272.

Sherman, L. and E. Cohen (1986). *Citizens Killed by Big City Police, 1970-1984*. Washington, D.C.: Crime Control Institute.

Uelmen, G. (1973). "Varieties of Police Policy: A Study of Police Policy Regarding the Use of Deadly Force in Los Angeles County." *Loyola Law Review*, 6:1-61.

Walker, S. (1977). *A Critical History of Police Reform*. Lexington, MA: Lexington Books.

Walker, S. (1980). *Popular Justice: A History of American Criminal Justice*. New York, NY: Oxford University Press.

Walker, S. (1986). "The Dynamics of Change in American Criminal Justice: Towards an Understanding of 'Reform'," in J. Kerner et al., (eds.), *European or North-American Juvenile Justice Systems—Aspects and Tendencies*. Munich.

Walker, S. (1988). *The Rule Revolution: Reflections on the Transformation of American Criminal Justice, 1950-1988*. Madison, WI: Institute for Legal Studies.

Wechsler, H. (1952). "The Challenge of a Model Penal Code." *Harvard Law Review*, 65(May):1097-1133.

Wilson, J. (1973). *Varieties of Police Behavior*. New York, NY: Antheneum.

Developing Police Policy: An Evaluation of the Control Principle

Geoffrey P. Alpert
University of South Carolina

William C. Smith
Sedgwick of the Carolinas

Law enforcement is a paradigm of operational control. Virtually every aspect of policing is subject to some combination of either law, policy, guideline, directive, rule or general order. By the very nature of the police function, such a tight rein appears to be critically necessary. Conventional wisdom is that police agencies must exercise strict control over their officers. As policing has become more complex there has been a tendency to overregulate the officers' actions. Creating complex policies, procedures and rules has become the customary method of controlling the discretion of police officers. It is the purpose of this paper to explore the context and role of police policy making and to address the need to authorize discretion rather than strictly control officers' behavior in many area of policing. The first section describes the legal parameters of policy and the differences among policies, procedures and rules. The second section reviews the areas that need strong policies and the areas that need only broad guidance. The third section includes a brief comment on the need to assess policies. The final section includes examples of the components of policy.

Legal Parameters of Policy

The primary mission of police is the protection of life. However, it would be naive to regard policy making as driven only by that altruistic principle. Other forces, including public preferences, the desire for uniform quality of performance and liability prevention all direct policy. Realistically, the police policy making process is governed by the principles of risk management and liability.

The history of policy making has been one of reaction. Traditionally, policies have been produced in a response to a problem. In recent years, however, policy makers have received a backhanded judicial incentive to review and revise their policies. When the U.S. Supreme Court in *City of Canton, Ohio v. Harris* (1989) recognized "deliberate indifference" as the benchmark for municipal policy deficiencies, it created a financial necessity for agencies to review, revise and sometimes develop policies (Alpert, 1989).

To understand the judicial incentive, a quick review of the history of police civil liability is necessary. Until the early 1960s, police civil liability was unremarkable and basically limited to claims of negligence (Kappeler, 1993 and del Carmen, 1991). The United States Supreme Court's decision in *Monroe v. Pape* (1961) had effectively alleviated concerns held by municipalities that they were proper defendants for citizens' civil rights claims brought under 42 U.S.C. Section 1983. This atmosphere continued until the Court's 1978 decision in *Monnell v. New York City Department of Social Services* (1978). The Court in *Monnell* effectively overruled *Pape* and opened the floodgates for Section 1983 actions against municipalities, thereby giving plaintiffs access to the deep pockets of the local treasury. The linchpin of the *Monnell* decision was that the policy of a municipality, as a moving force behind a plaintiff's injury, could result in municipal liability. In essence, the courts were evaluating the behavior of the police and were involved in judicial rule making (Alpert and Haas, 1984). Since *Monnell,* additional refinements of the 'policy' rule have resulted in municipal liability concerns regarding police 'custom' and 'practice.'

Noteworthy among these refinements are cases which have held that an elected county prosecuting attorney who provided advice to the police is a "policy maker" of a county for purposes of attaching liability (*Pembaur v. City of Cincinnati,* 1986) and one in which an unchecked pattern of violence was held to be attributable to a sheriff's policy of inadequate training (*Davis v. Mason County,* 1991).

Although local municipalities have been put under great pressure to address policy issues, state agencies and their employees have felt some sense of insulation from the threat of lawsuits brought pursuant to Section 1983. This belief has persisted even through the Supreme Court's enthronement of the 'deliberate indifference' standard in *City of Canton v. Harris* (1989). The sense of security was brought about by the ostensible protection of the Eleventh Amendment which precludes suits against states in a federal court and by judicial interpretations that extended the protection to federally created causes of action that could be brought in state court. Indeed, the Supreme Court held as recently as 1989 in *Will v. Michigan Department of State Police* that state actors in their official capacities enjoyed immunity from suit under Section 1983 even when brought in state court. Prior to *Will,* the holding in *Howlett v. Rose* (1987) conferred the same immunity in federal court Section 1983 actions. As a result of this reasoning, state law enforcement officials and their officials have enjoyed greater immunity than their local law enforcement counterparts in Section 1983 cases where "official capacity" actions have been involved.

The 1990s, however, have brought about a rethinking of the status of such immunity. In *Hafer v. Melo* (1991), the United States Supreme Court allowed an elected official to be sued under Section 1983 for what were alleged by her to be 'official capacity' actions. The significance of the case lies in its discussion of the distinctions between actions taken in a personal capacity and those performed in official capacity. The operational consequence of the case is pressure on all law enforcement executives to review their various methods of control, including policies, lest such control methods be deemed to constitute personal capacity actions.

Policies, Procedures and Rules

A *policy* is not a statement of what must be done in a particular situation but it is a statement of guiding principles that must be followed in activities that fall within either specific organizational objectives or the overall police mission. A policy is a guide to thinking. A *procedure* is the method of performing a task or a manner of proceeding on a course of action. It differs from policy in that it specifies action in a particular situation to perform a task within the guidelines of policy. A procedure is a guide to action. A *rule* is a managerial mandate that either requires or prohibits specified behavior. A rule is a mandate to action. These various control mechanisms are designed to address a multitude of needs, including the need for regulation and uniformity of police activities.

The National Advisory Commission on Criminal Justice Standards and Goals, *Report on Police* (1973:54) provides an excellent discussion of the differences among written policies, procedures and rules.

> Policy is different from rules and procedures. Policy should be stated in broad terms to guide employees. It sets limits of discretion. A policy statement deals with the principles and values that guide the performance of activities directed toward the achievement of agency objectives. A procedure is a way of proceeding—a routine—to achieve an objective. Rules significantly reduce or eliminate discretion by specifically stating what must and must not be done.

As an example, this notion has been translated by the Metro-Dade Police Department in Miami, Florida which has defined policy as, ". . . principles and values which guide the performance of a departmental activity. Policy is not a statement of what must be done in a particular situation; rather, it is a statement of guiding principles which should be followed in activities which are directed toward attainment of objectives" (1989:5).

These directives, in varying degrees, establish discretionary parameters for officers to perform day-to-day operations in a manner consistent with the philosophy of the administration and command staff. Policies, based upon relevant laws and philosophy, serve to control officers' behavioral choices.

The Need for Control in Police Activities

Law enforcement agencies must have rules, regulations, training, supervision and structured accountability to guide and control the broad discretionary powers of their officers. However, as officers are confronted daily with a variety of complex situations, discretion is necessary (Adams, 1990). Discretion must be guided by legal strictures and administrative philosophy rather than by adrenaline-charged, split-second decisions. Written and enforced directives are necessary for the proper management of law enforcement functions because of the structural, personal and situational factors that affect behavioral choices. These directives are formulated by determining objectives and identifying the principles or ideas that will best guide the officer in achieving them (Alpert and Dunham, 1992).

The objectives and methods of police departments are affected by the laws, the communities they serve, their parent political system, the fraternal associations, unions, professional police associations and other general and special interest groups (Sheehan and Cordner, 1989:465). A policy indicates to the officers and the public the agency's philosophy in the area of concern and also provides a set of standards by which it can be held accountable (see Alpert and Dunham, 1992). As James Auten (1988:1-2) has noted:

> To do otherwise is to simply leave employees "in the Dark" in the expectation that they will intuitively divine the proper and expected course of action in the performance of their duties . . . Discretion must be reasonably exercised within the parameters of the expectations of the community, the courts, the legislature and the organization, itself.

Similarly, Robert Wasserman informs us (1982:40):

> . . . When written policy statements are not available (or not well disseminated), the police agency and the administration run considerable risk that some police actions will be completely alien to a segment of the community. This result can be aggra-

> vated conflict between police and the community, resulting in political demands for major measures to ensure accountability on the part of the police organization.

Wasserman warns the police administrators to create and disseminate policy directives before a problem occurs and the public holds the police and other government officials accountable. Policies and procedures must cover general duties and obligations as well as methods to achieve them. In other words, law enforcement agencies must have regulations, provide training and supervision and hold officers accountable for their actions.

Deciding upon which activities and tasks require strong control or fundamental guidance requires a comprehensive understanding of the role and function of police in society. One aspect of that insight is the increasing educational level of the police. During the past few years, more educated persons are joining the police force and many officers are raising their level of education. At a time when police are becoming more educated, the requirements of the police are becoming more complicated. No longer do the police simply respond to calls for service. The renewed emphasis on community-oriented policing and problem-solving policing requires officers to think and plan rather than just respond (Alpert and Dunham, 1992). That is, officers are being educated and trained to use good judgment and discretion in many situations. However, in some critical areas, officers need strong policies and training.

Identification of Policy Areas

There is little doubt that some police activities require closer supervision and control than others. Although much of the police function may occur in areas of high public visibility, neither logic nor necessity mandate that every activity or decision be subject to strict agency directive or control. The crucial task is to identify those behaviors that should be value-driven and those that must be control-driven. Obviously, behavior which, if improperly carried out, is likely to result in severe injury or death, must be subject to control-driven policies.

David LaBrec (1982) has designed a graphic that helps to explain the categories of risk. Simply put, the police functions that are high-risk and low frequency require strong policies, formal procedures and explicit rules. The high-frequency, low-risk functions can be discharged with minimal guidance and a strong system of shared values (see Greene et al., 1992). The use of force or deadly force can be considered a high-risk, low-frequency activity, and police pursuit driving can be considered a high-risk, high-frequency activity (Alpert and Fridell, 1992). These functions require the most extensive policies, training and overall guidance (Alpert and Smith, 1991).

Figure 1
Categories of Risk

	Frequency: High	Frequency: Low
Exposure: High	High Frequency High Exposure	Low Frequency High Exposure
Exposure: Low	High Frequency Low Exposure	Low Frequency Low Exposure

There are police activities that require specific direction but not to the extent required for use of deadly force or pursuit driving. In fact, some of these activities if subjected to a strict control policy may result in officer behavior which is detached, dispassionate or cold. For example, police response to domestic violence incidents requires not only tact but the ability to read a situation and respond in the interests of all parties. Such a complicated behavioral scenario would be virtually impossible to regulate by a strict control policy. However, certain important procedural issues must be controlled by this type of policy, including statutory requirements concerning the timing and substance of the police response to a domestic abuse call, arrest requirements as well as the coordination of efforts among officers, investigators and victim service agencies (Buzawa and Buzawa, 1992).

Many of these police tasks must be considered as an art, requiring a fluid response and not a mechanical reaction. Policing requires a variety of behavioral alternatives. That is, officers need wide discretion in those areas of their work not directly and immediately involved in the protection of life or defense against injury. Discretion must not be based on 'gut reaction' or a whim, but requires extensive quality pre-service and in-service training. In order for officers to choose an appropriate response (discretionary choice), he or she must be trained in the options available. A critical part of the training must focus on ethics, values and morals. Value-driven guidelines are preferred in areas not directly involved in the protection of life or defense against injury (Greene et al., 1992).

An example of a police function requiring only summary guidance is telephone contact with the public. Police administrators have no need to instruct their officers and civilians who answer the telephone to read a written statement. They should, however, require officers to be pleasant, cooperative and provide assistance. Further, a policy in this area should direct the officer or civilian to collect certain information. The Metro-Dade Police Department (1989:32) provides the following direction:

> **Telephone Communications:** The telephone is the primary method by which police services are requested. All incoming telephone calls must be answered promptly to provide the desired quality of service.
>
> **Telephone Courtesy:** When answering the telephone, an employee should identify the unit and himself, and ask to be of assistance. Employees should make every attempt to supply requested information and assistance or refer party to proper agency.

Answering the telephone is a high-frequency, low-risk function. Obviously, officer discretion is important as long as it fits within the general guidelines of the agency. The examples of force, response to domestic violence and answering the telephone establish points on a policy-control continuum.

Figure 2
Continuum of Policy

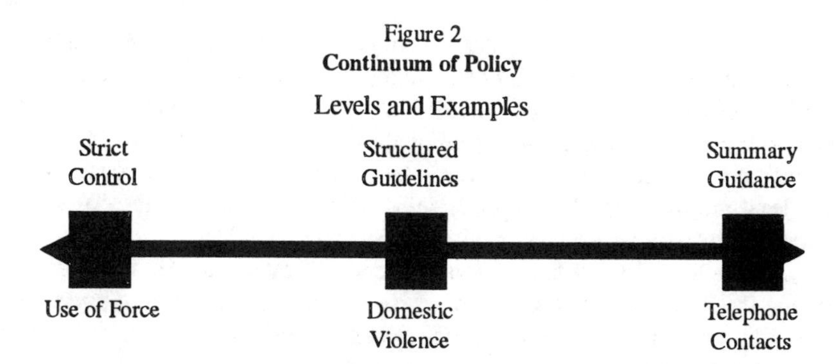

Police agencies must determine which functions require the most stringent control and which require structured guidelines or summary guidance only. Using examples discussed above, Figure 2 provides an illustration of the continuum of policy control.

A valuable example of this determination process can be taken from private industry. Private companies are increasingly minimizing formal rules and placing importance on value training and discretionary behavior (Cordner, 1989). Moore and Stephens (1991) suggest more reliance on what Kenneth Andrews labeled "The Corporate Strategy" (Andrews, 1980). This strategy refers to the identification of an objective(s), design of the organizational character and allocation of resources to achieve the objectives under potentially adverse circumstances. While there are numerous differences between the public and private sectors which complicate the transfer of technology and operational philosophies, private enterprise offers an innovative direction worthy of analysis (Cordner, 1989 and Moore and Stephens, 1991).

Concepts derived from the private sector transferred to police management would raise the following issues. Officer discretion is appropriate if defensible and valid hiring and fitness-for-duty evaluations are employed. Focus in training should be shifted to allow officers greater creativity in dealing with "non-textbook" scenarios where human emotion, pride or dignity are at issue. It is critical that police officers learn to deal with members of the public as fellow human beings rather than as participants in situations. It is necessary not to program an officer's response to a preconceived scenario but permit a response that incorporates training and preparation. In other words, the control principle must not be permitted to escape its bounds and take reason and compassion hostage. Perhaps the area of policing in which there is the greatest need for control is the use of force.

An Example of Force

In 1970, Egon Bittner noted that the unique feature of the police is their power to use force and deadly force limited only by law and policy. Further, the significance of this power, he argued, includes its omnipresent potential and threat. No other occupational group possesses this authority. Although police use of physical force is not a frequent event, its abuse is by any human means irreversible and by any legal means incapable of compensation. In other words, it is the classic low-frequency, high-risk event (see Friedrich, 1980 and Fyfe, 1988).

Although a relatively low-frequency event, accusations of excessive force are among the most common and highly visible complaints made against police officers. The proliferation of control mechanisms in this and other areas has been fueled by the nature and ever-increasing number of civil liability actions filed against the police (i.e., Rodney King). The absence of meaningful policy and training in critical function areas may serve as an invitation to sue where the absence is proximately related to a plaintiff's injury. Other explanations for increased control range from the traditional and generalized perception of need by the command staff to specific needs including administrative discipline and the accreditation movement. In effect, it could be safely said that the extent of policy within a police agency is linked to the intensity of its mission and its potential exposure to liability. In sum, the police who are given the authority to use force over others must be subject to significant restraint in its application.

Officer discretion must be guided by implementing a structured policy and providing extensive and continuous training to remove the need to make split-second decisions. This discretion may be cultivated by the following strategies: the articulation and acceptance of organizational values, internal inspections and audits of incidents, community feedback, an interactive style of policing and an appropriate system of discipline (Alpert and Dunham, 1992 and Alpert and Fridell, 1992).

An unintended consequence of strict control policies, however, is their expansion into areas where such structure may be disadvantageous to both law enforcement and the public it serves (Cordner, 1989). Cordner notes that "The prevailing wisdom in modern police administration is that policies and rules are needed to govern every contingency and every substantial aspect of operation and management" (1989:17). The critical question becomes: Is a strict-control policy model effective for all behavior or has the current trend of developing policies for most police functions set forth on a faulty premise?

Proposing Boundary Limitations

As discussed above, the use of deadly force may be low-frequency but is high-risk. The current paranoia over civil liability and the need to improve relations with members of the community have caused many police agencies to implement a strong system of oversight and superficial accountability of daily police operations. On the one hand, some policy makers, by addressing each important police function, believe that they are insulated from personal or institutional liability. On the other hand, some believe this strategy merely decreases officers' discretion without any corresponding immunity (see del Carmen, 1991). From either position, a strong-control form of management ignores a critical aspect of the police function: human interaction. Further, a program of extensive regulation by policy likely conveys to officers a message of distrust and engenders a stifling of creativity. The critical issue is to identify the acceptable limits for strict-control mechanisms.

Proposed boundaries may be drawn at those activities that are oriented to *protection of life* and *defense against injury*. While the principal mission of the police is the protection of life, not every activity in the duty day is directed toward this goal. A useful inquiry in identifying those police functions that are life-preserving and that defend against injury is accomplished by asking whether the activity involved will likely cause severe injury or death if improperly discharged. In other words, a behavioral threshold should be created so that, once crossed, strict control would be appropriate. This concept, in its purest sense, should create little controversy; for it is precisely the approach that is underscored in the majority of police agencies. For example, few would argue with the view that the discharge of a firearm, vehicular pursuit of an offender, or the use of a baton or Taser must be subject to strenuous control. The stark reality is that such behaviors are relatively infrequent although their criticality is great. What is proposed is that police officers be afforded the opportunity in less than critical areas, such as the ones mentioned above, to participate in a belief system where their discretionary actions reflect a legitimate desire to serve the public.

Recently, Cohen and Feldberg (1991:148-149) identified three factors that provide police officers with sufficient information to operate successfully in a law-enforcement agency.

> The practical ingredients and individual needs in order to have free moral choice in matters of professional conduct are an understanding of the values that inform his or her profession, the intention to live up to the values and an environment that supports those values and discourages behavior that is contrary to them.

Basically, appropriate departmental policies, training and a powerful accountability or disciplinary system will create an environment that establishes the mission and philosophy of the agency. If an officer is trained in those values and guidelines and chooses to follow them, he or she will be able to use discretion appropriately. Hopefully, this training and understanding will help officers make the appropriate behavioral choices and mirror what Cohen and Feldberg have called the "free moral choice in matters of professional conduct" (1991:148).

Assessing the Effectiveness of Policies

Police officers perform a wide variety of functions and the agencies in which they work are traditionally organized in a paramilitary structure with a specific chain-of-command. This structure and function suggests a need for a strong-control type of management. The evolution of many policy manuals is based upon the negative reinforcement of behavior. Many policy directives are stated negatively and it is often difficult to measure their effectiveness as police performance measures are typically based upon positive behaviors. The difference between what is measurable and the behavior recommended by the majority of policies creates serious "bean-counting" or methodological problems for evaluation (see Spelman, 1988). As Cordner notes (1989:19), "No experiments have been conducted to test the effectiveness of written rules and guidelines. There simply is not much agreement about how to define or measure the effectiveness of a police agency."

Rather than evaluate the effectiveness of a proposed policy, many administrators have made policy changes as a response to officers' mistakes. This process has created in many agencies a compilation of guidelines, regulations and rules that prohibit behavior that has been found inappropriate or in violation of the law. Some aspects of policy or a rule may be attributed to a specific officer or situation. Often, these rules are fondly named after the officer or event.

While this approach appears solid, it creates a situation that may be too limiting and challenges officers to circumvent the language of the policy. In other words, control-oriented management can lead to a macro-management approach by always limiting behavioral alternatives with rules.

A superficial assessment of this 'prohibition' approach may yield a positive result. However, an in-depth analysis would likely come to a different conclusion. The consequences of the approach are a loss of police services, reduced morale among the officers and an environment that stifles creative police work. Gary Cordner notes (1989:18):

> The question of most importance is whether extensive written directives make police organizations more effective. Do rules and regulations improve the quality of police service? Do they contribute to police goal attainment?

These questions raise very important issues that remain unanswered. The next section addresses the elements that should be included in an appropriate and defensible policy.

Elements of Model Policies

The development of police policies should reflect the values of the command staff *and community* and should include input from officers at all levels. Policies should incorporate the following principles:

1. Be workable in real-world situations;
2. be adaptable to training;
3. be written in a positive manner;
4. refer to or incorporate relevant laws;
5. be pre-tested to assure that all officers understand the specific intent and consequences of non-compliance;
6. include in-service training, as a matter of record, for all officers and supervisors; and
7. provide examples of behavior.

Many departmental policies have been developed properly, include these principles and provide excellent direction and guidance to their officers. Other agencies do not have policies or have such weak policies that they provide no real direction. As a response to the problems of developing and refining policies, the International Association of Chiefs of Police (IACP) established a National Law Enforcement Policy Center. Through the auspices of the Center, the IACP developed the most comprehensive compilation of model policies and background papers (Issues and Concepts) justifying their views (National Law Enforcement Policy Center, 1991). This compilation includes policies on some of the most difficult issues facing law enforcement in the 1990s. The model policies include protection of life issues with little discretion such as the use of force, deadly force and pursuit driving as well as areas permitting wide discretion such as a policy to control a confidential fund.

The model policies were developed to provide general guidance. A disclaimer states that the models must be reviewed and adjusted to individual departments. The requirement to adjust these models must be emphasized. Different jurisdictions and environments need different direction to produce the best policing. However, any agency would benefit from the outline and background papers prepared by the Policy Center. Fortunately, there are many commonalities among police policies for high-risk activities. These include a policy's *first* principle, that an officers' primary responsibility is to protect lives. As many police activities are potentially dangerous and because officers are likely to react to the heat of the moment, an overall *MISSION STATEMENT* must be included as a first element and as a reminder in policies guiding high-risk activities. Beyond the mission statement, the IACP models provide an excellent design for developing an agency's policy. For example, the model policy regarding use of force is detailed and includes the following headings or elements:

A. Purpose
B. Policy (statement of philosophy)
C. Definitions
D. Procedures
   1. parameters for use of deadly force;
   2. parameters for the use of nondeadly force;
   3. training and qualifications;
   4. reporting uses of force; and
   5. departmental response (administrative review).

By adding a mission statement to this outline, a department will have an excellent foundation for a policy. It is important to acknowledge the threat that new policies may have on some departments' officers.

If a new philosophy is incorporated in a policy or a more structured response is required from an officer, effective training to the policy is required. Effective training may include the reading, understanding and discussion of a policy for low-risk activities. However, in high-risk activities, beyond the understanding of the language of the policy, practice and simulation or role-playing decision-making skills may be necessary to avoid what the United States Supreme Court has called, "deliberate indifference."

Accountability

Just as police policies are divided among several levels based upon their consequences, accountability of officers must also be structured. Officers who make contact with citizens are usually asked to take notes on the meeting to preserve any information that was provided. Officers who are involved in automobile accidents will have to complete a mandated accident reporting form. Officers who must control a suspect with force to effect an arrest should be responsible for completing a "control of persons" report. If deadly force is used, an officer must complete a form describing the why, where and how. It is important to hold accountable any officer who has been involved in some low-risk and all high-risk activities. Writing an analytical critique is the first step. This process serves several purposes: ***first,*** the information contained in a critique can help determine if the action was necessary and conducted within the departmental policy; ***second,*** critiques will help determine if specific training is needed; ***third,*** critiques will help determine if a change in policy is needed; and ***fourth,*** an analysis of the data generated in these reports will reveal trends and demonstrate specific risk factors. As a second step, the agency must assign supervisory personnel to evaluate these reports and determine if a violation has occurred and suggest that the officer face disciplinary action.

An agency's disciplinary system is a critical reinforcer of its policies and rules. It is important that an agency's policies are followed and that an appropriate disciplinary scheme is established for violations. An important function of the disciplinary action is the message that is sent to others when an officer is disciplined or when he or she is *not* disciplined for a policy violation. All officers must understand the importance of the rules and regulations and the consequences for violating them. For example, if an officer is involved in a preventable accident, it is important to have a disciplinary scheme established. The first violation may result in a letter to the file while a second violation may require some remedial training. A third violation may result in a change of duty so the individual does not have an opportunity to use force to control a suspect. At some point a department will have to take more drastic action and those steps must also be made known to the officers. A policy without a disciplinary system will not be taken as seriously as one which includes a system of discipline. Similarly, a disciplinary system that can be subverted or manipulated will not serve as a deterrent. There is no room for "winking" at a violation and excusing poor judgment or deliberate actions which results in a violation of policy.

This concept has been summarized by The United States Commission on Civil Rights which found that (1981:158):

> Once a finding sustains the allegation of wrongdoing, disciplinary sanctions commensurate with the seriousness of the offense

that are imposed fairly, swiftly, and consistently will most clearly reflect the commitment of the department to oppose police misconduct. Less severe action such as reassignment, retraining, and psychological counseling may be appropriate in some cases.

Conclusion

Creating meaningful mechanisms of control, including the development of police policies is a process of integrating a wide variety of interests. To be effective, policy must address the legitimate concerns of the public as well as the law. In balancing these issues, due attention must be paid to future flexibility and the process of refinement and change.

Police activities range from low-criticality to high-criticality and low-frequency to high-frequency. Police officials must identify which activities require strict control-oriented policies and which require only summary guidance. In other words, the style of policy will vary according to a continuum of control. In addition, there must be training to the policy, control and supervision of the activities and a system of discipline that holds the officers and agency accountable for the behavior.

The determination of the type of policy to be employed in any given duty function must be based upon the command staff's realization and understanding of law enforcement as a service to the public. Investiture of discretion to officers in low criticality areas after proper training in ethics, values and morals may go a great distance in bridging intermittent gaps between the police and the community. By the same token, high criticality functions will necessitate strict-control policies to guide them to protect the public safely in an effective and efficient manner.

References

Adams, T. (1990). *Police Field Operations.* Englewood Cliffs, NJ: Prentice-Hall.

Alpert, G. (1989). "*City of Canton v. Harris* and the Deliberate Indifference Standard." *Criminal Law Bulletin,* 25: 466-472 .

Alpert, G. and R. Dunham (1992). *Policing Urban America.* Prospect Heights, IL: Waveland Press.

Alpert, G. and L. Fridell (1992). *Police Vehicles and Firearms: Instruments of Deadly Force.* Prospect Heights, IL: Waveland Press.

Alpert, G. and K. Haas (1984). "Judicial Rulemaking and the Fourth Amendment: Cars, Containers and Exclusionary Justice." *Alabama Law Review,* 35: 23-61.

Alpert, G. and W. Smith (1991). "Beyond City Limits and into the Wood(s): A Brief Look at the Policy Implications of *City of Canton v. Harris* and *Wood v. Ostrander*." *American Journal of Police*, 10:19-40.

Andrews, K. (1980). *The Concept of Corporate Strategy.* Chicago, IL: Irwin.

Auten, J. (1988). "Preparing Written Guidelines." *FBI Law Enforcement Bulletin*, 57:1-7.

Bittner, E. (1970). *The Functions of Police in Modern Society.* Rockville, MD: National Institute of Mental Health.

Brooks, L. (1989). "Police Discretionary Behavior: A Study of Style." In R. Dunham and G. Alpert (eds.), *Critical Issues in Policing.* Prospect Heights, IL: Waveland Press.

Brown, M. (1981). *Working the Street: Police Discretion and the Dilemmas of Reform.* New York, NY: Russell Sage Foundation.

Buzawa, E. and C. Buzawa (1992). *Domestic Violence: The Criminal Justice Response.* New York, NY: Greenwood Press.

Cohen, H. and M. Feldberg (1991). *Power and Restraint: The Moral Dimension of Police Work.* Westport, CT: Praeger.

Cordner, G. (1989). "Written Rules and Regulations: Are They Necessary?: *FBI Law Enforcement Bulletin*, July:17-21.

Davis, K. (1975). *Police Discretion.* St. Paul, MN: West Publishing.

del Carmen, R. (1991). *Civil Liabilities in American Policing.* Englewood Cliffs, NJ: Brady.

Friedrich, R. (1980). "Police Use of Force: Individuals, Situations and Organizations." *Annals of the American Academy of Political and Social Science*, 452:82-97.

Fyfe, J. (1988). *The Metro-Dade Police—Citizen Violence Reduction Project.* Washington, DC: Police Foundation.

Greene, J., G. Alpert, and P. Styles. "Values and Culture in Two American Police Departments: Lessons from King Arthur." *Contemporary Criminal Justice*, 8:183-207.

LaBrec, D. (1982). "Risk Management: Preventive Law Practice and Practical Risk Management Methods for the 1980s." Paper presented to the Annual Meeting of the National Institute of Municipal Law Officers, Miami, FL.

Kappeler, V. (1993). *Critical Issues in Police Civil Liability.* Prospect Heights, IL: Waveland Press.

Metro-Dade Police Department (1989). *Metro-Dade Police Department Manual—Part 1.* Dade County Florida.

Moore, M. and D. Stephens (1991). *Beyond Command and Control: The Strategic Management of Police Departments.* Washington, DC: Police Executive Research Forum.

National Advisory Commission on Criminal Justice Standards and Goals (1973). *Report on Police.* Washington, DC: U.S. Government Printing Office.

National Law Enforcement Policy Center (1991). *A Compilation of Model Policies.* Arlington, VA: National Law Enforcement Policy Center.

Sheehan, R. and G. Cordner (1989). *Introduction to Police Management.* Cincinnati, OH: Anderson Publishing Co.

Spelman, W. (1988). *Beyond Bean Counting.* Washington, D.C.: Police Executive Research Forum.

United States Commission on Civil Rights (1981). *Who is Guarding the Guardians?* Washington, DC: U.S. Government Printing Office.

Wasserman, R. (1982). "Government Setting." In B. Garmire (ed.), *Local Government Police Management. Second Edition.* Washington, DC: International City Management Association.

Cases

City of Canton, Ohio v. Harris, 489 U.S. 378 (1989).
Davis v. Mason County, 927 F.2d 1473 (9th Cir. 1991).
Monroe v. Pape, 365 U.S. 167 (1961).
Monnell v. New York City Department of Social Services, 436 U.S. 658 (1978).
Pembaur v. City of Cincinnati, 475 U.S. 469 (1986).
Will v. Michigan Department of State Police, 491 U.S. 58 (1990).
Howlett v. Rose, 469 U.S. 356 (1990).

Section III

Performance and Accountability

Introduction

Among the key issues in police administration are the definition of good police performance (what should officers do?), the measurement of performance (of individuals, units, and the entire agency), and the meaning of police accountability (who should be held responsible, and for what?). These issues go directly to the heart of the police role and to our conceptions of good police work—matters over which there is considerable disagreement and controversy. To some degree these issues are timeless and intractable; they come to the forefront with even greater than usual urgency, though, when society and the police profession are considering new models of policing. Such is the case today with respect to community policing.

In the first article in this section, Tim Oettmeier and Mary Ann Wycoff report on the proceedings of a conference of police practitioners that considered performance issues connected to community policing. As they note, "(r)evision of performance evaluation to reflect the diverse responsibilities of an ever broadening police role is something many managers still need to accomplish in the 1990s." On the plus side (from the standpoint of encouraging change), nearly all police personnel, both officers and managers, seem dissatisfied with their current systems for evaluating performance. On the down side, though, conference participants reached no strong consensus about how to improve police performance measurement systems.

Oettmeier and Wycoff discuss many of the difficult issues that impinge on police performance measurement and describe the range of practices currently used in police departments. Among other things, they conclude that police officials need to be clear about the *purpose* of any performance measurement system (e.g., for feedback to police officers versus for pay determinations); that individual "grading" must be based more on effort than on effect (since so many problems are beyond the direct control of individual officers and are susceptible to uncontrollable and unpredictable external influences); that unit objectives need to be tied more clearly to overall organizational goals; that, insofar as possible, *simplicity* should characterize performance measurement and evaluation systems; and that concern for employees as well as for the organization should guide the design of such systems. Perhaps most importantly, they found that "performance measurement, like community policing itself, needs to be tailored to the characteristics of the agency and the community it serves."

Philip Rhoades, in his article subtitled "Connecting Police Ethics and Democratic Values," takes a different approach to questions about the police role and proper police behavior. He takes this approach within a consideration of police ethics, a topic that has drawn increasing attention over the past decade or so. Policing and police administration have always included ethical choices, problems, and dilemmas, of course. What has changed recently is the willingness of police officials to acknowledge some of the ethical issues inherent in policing, and an increasing interest in these issues among police scholars, philosophers, and ethicists.

Rhoades argues that "police should be viewed, not as traditional professionals, but as public agents within representative bureaucracies with clear political obligations." His qualms about policing as a profession are not new; there has been an ongoing debate for years over whether police work should be considered an art, a craft, a profession, or something else. His main concern, though, is that recent interest in police ethics has tended to be limited to a "professional ethics" framework. In Rhoades' view, this limited approach tends to distract attention from some fundamental considerations underlying policing in a free society; in particular, that policing must adhere to democratic values and democratic processes. This is an extremely important insight that is so fundamental, so basic, that we have a tendency to overlook it when making decisions about proper police behavior, how to measure it, and how to hold individual police officers and police organizations accountable.

The final article in this section, and in the book, takes a look at what the future might hold for police administration. Jack Enter outlines ten trends in society, in crime, and in management that are likely to cause changes in (or problems for) police organizations and police management. Significant social trends that he foresees include the aging of the population, cultural diversification, and the expanding roles of women. Crime trends include more older offenders, more older victims, fewer youthful offenders (but not necessarily less youth crime), and more female offenders. Management trends relate to personnel diversification, older employees, and new management philosophies.

Enter concludes as follows:

> many of the present philosophies and operational policies of law enforcement agencies will gradually become less able to cope with a world that is even more complex and dynamic than the one that exists today. Our criminal justice system has often been accused of being slow to respond to change. In the future, this hesitancy to embrace change may be more damaging than in the past.

Those of you reading this article in the future (if you are reading it in the past, we'd really like to hear from you) can judge for yourselves whether the world did change as Enter predicted, whether police organizations adapted well or poorly, and whether the consequences of hesitant adaptation were as dire as he thought.

Police Performance in the Nineties: Practitioner Perspectives

Timothy N. Oettmeier
Houston Police Department

Mary Ann Wycoff
Police Foundation

The redesign of performance measurement is once again on the agenda of police managers. Twenty years ago, a report from the Dallas Police Department stated:

> In the past, performance evaluation in the police department has been a largely meaningless biannual exercise in numerically grading employees with little thought to the true purpose of performance evaluation (Dallas Police Department, 1972, p. III-23,24).

Since this was written, Dallas has changed substantially its own employee evaluation process, but this statement could be made today by too many other police agencies. In Houston, for example, the evaluation process currently in place was designed over forty years ago. In departments all over the country, officers commonly complain about the irrelevance of performance measurement. Complaints range from criticisms about the subjectivity of the process to the fact that it may have little bearing on pay raises, assignments, or promotions.

Measurement of agency performance also is an issue. Criteria to determine agency effectiveness seldom are established. Traditional standards of response time, crime rates, and arrest rates continue to be offered as benchmarks with which the public should assess agency accomplishments. While important, the inadequacy of these indicators as comprehensive measures of agency performance has been widely acknowledged.

The 1972 Dallas report was prompted by an organizational initiative to reexamine and reshape the police role with the goal of rewarding officers for the provision of a wider range of police services than traditionally had been the case. In this decade, the philosophy of community policing is moving perhaps hundreds of departments similarly to question the effectiveness of various organizational systems.

Unless these systems are altered to support the evolving roles and responsibilities associated with this philosophy, organizational change will be thwarted—stopped dead in its tracks—without a fair test. Most critical among the roles affected by a community policing approach is that of patrol officers.

Community Policing, Neighborhood Oriented Policing (NOP) and Problem Oriented Policing (POP) all encourage officers to exercise more discretion and work with community representatives to tailor responses to meet a variety of needs existing within local communities. Officers' responsibilities will vary in accordance with where they work and the time of day or night they work. They should be prepared to respond to calls for service, interdict criminal activity through the deployment of proactive, tactical strategies, and develop coactive partnerships with local residents and business proprietors as a means of devising strategic approaches to complex crime and disorder issues. Executives can facilitate this role change by redesigning the process and criteria of performance measurement to convey the appropriate performance expectations to their officers.

Performance Measurement in the Community Policing Context

The issues that characterize performance analysis in a community policing context are much like those in any police setting. The need for assessment procedures to be valid, legal, reliable, useful, and equitable (see Mastrofski and Wadman, 1991) is the same, regardless of organizational philosophy. Meeting these requirements is a difficult task given the high probability of conflicts among them. The goal of equity, for example, may conflict with the goal of validity. When jobs are dissimilar within patrol because of geographical assignment or duty time, the need for equity may reduce the evaluated job dimensions to the most common elements of the role. This could result in an evaluation that fails to reflect any officer's actual job responsibilities.

Concerns for both legality and reliability have pushed departments toward quantifiable performance indicators. The increased emphasis administrators placed on the crime fighting aspects of the police role in previous decades (Kelling and Moore, 1988) also created pressure for quantifiable measures. The indicators that were most readily available were those associated (even if spuriously) with crime fighting (e.g., rapid response, numbers of arrests, etc.) and with organizational regulations (e.g., tardiness, sick time taken, accidents, etc.) (See Kelling, 1992). When important behaviors or activities cannot be counted, then the ones that are counted tend to become those that are considered important (Wycoff, 1982a). The emphases on the crime function and on quantitative assessments have led to performance assessments that overlook as much as seventy percent of the police role (Wycoff, 1982b).[1]

Revision of performance evaluation to reflect the diverse responsibilities of an ever broadening police role is something many managers still need to accomplish in the 1990s, regardless of whether they have any interest in changing their organization's current approach to policing. Changes in policing philosophies only make more apparent the need for managers to acknowledge and support activities effective officers always have conducted but which have gone officially unrecognized.

Changes in officers' roles are necessarily accompanied by changes in the roles of managers and supervisors; and these changes extend beyond the evaluation function. Official expansion of the officer's role will require sergeants, for example, to support the use of, and to hold officers accountable for, the greater discretion they are permitted.

To support the work of officers, sergeants will need to become more efficient managers, team builders, and group facilitators. Sergeants should develop the capacity to build resource capabilities for their officers. They should be an active participant in devising more global approaches to addressing problems of crime and disorder. And, of critical importance, is their ability to sense and interpret local opportunities for, and hindrances to, action being taken by the officers.

Weisburd, McElroy and Hardyman (1989) suggest that the paramilitary model of policing facilitates close supervision of the officers' traditional role but is inappropriate for the broader, more discretionary[2] role of the community police officer (see also Goldstein, 1979 and Bittner, 1980). While it is debatable how many sergeants effectively "supervise" their officers in departments that restrict what officers are allowed to do, it is clear that community policing will require a reformulation of the sergeant's role that corresponds with changes in the responsibilities of the officers.

To accomplish this, sergeants, like officers, will need to seek more effective means of getting information from the community. Generally, the only "significant" form of feedback from the citizenry has been in the form of complaints about improper police activity. Notwithstanding the importance of attending to citizen complaints, departments need to collect data about services citizens want and about whether citizens believe their service needs are being met. A number of strategies have been advocated for accomplishing this. Numerous departments have used community meetings as a forum for eliciting service needs and preferences (e.g., the Positive Interaction Program in Houston). Some have employed door-to-door surveys conducted by officers (e.g., Grand Rapids, Michigan; Houston, Texas; Newark, New Jersey). A few departments with substantial resources (usually provided with grants) have conducted scientific community surveys. The Madison, Wisconsin Police Department routinely surveys, by mail, a sample of all citizens who have received service from the department in an effort to measure satisfaction and to collect information about ways of improving service.

In addition to recognizing the value of community feedback, community policing has also caused some administrators to question the appropriateness of individual employee evaluations. Some departments are emphasizing a focus on the team or workgroup rather than the individual. Those that retain individual evaluations may abandon them as a means of differentiating among employees for the purpose of rewards and, instead, use the individual evaluations as a means of helping individual employees identify and meet their own career goals (Gabor, 1992).

The Madison, Wisconsin and Houston, Texas police departments, for example, while having parallel goals of pursuing community policing and decentralization, have taken different approaches to individual performance evaluation. Madison has, at least for the present, abandoned individual evaluations until a more appropriate process can be developed. In the meantime, the organization is emphasizing the improvement of organizational systems (including management) and the development of teamwork.

In Madison, discussions of performance focus on changes or improvements that need to be made in order to support the work of officers in the field. Evaluations of managers are made by employees who respond to questions about the changes the manager needs to make in order for the employee to function more effectively. These critiques are for the purpose of information gathering rather than "grading," and they are used by managers for self-diagnosis.

Patrol officers in Madison's Experimental (or South) Police District receive evaluations directly from citizens. The survey that the department mails to service recipients is returned directly to the officer who delivered the service. The identity of the citizen is not known, but the officer has general information about the type of situation on which the evaluation is based. Officers decide whether to share their personal evaluations with peers and supervisors. After reading the survey response, the officer removes his identification from the form and gives it to the supervisor. The individual responses are then aggregated to determine whether the district as a whole is meeting citizen expectations.

At a similar stage in its own redirection of philosophy, the Houston Police Department invested significant effort in redesigning individual performance evaluations so they would reflect the enhanced job responsibilities officers were now being encouraged to perform. Houston, like many other departments, does not have the same legal latitude as Madison to eliminate individual performance evaluations. More importantly, Houston managers view performance evaluation as a critical support system to be used to communicate and reinforce management expectations associated with the organization's philosophy. Like Madison, Houston, via its research efforts, experimented with having officers evaluate their immediate supervisors and with having citizens participate in the evaluation process of police officer performance. Houston and Madison are only two examples of departments that share a similar policing philosophy, but are taking different approaches toward the performance measurement issue.

Neighborhood-Oriented Policing in Houston

By 1987, the Houston Police Department had developed a commitment to Neighborhood-Oriented Policing (NOP). The concept was being operationalized within three of the City's twenty master police districts involving over 300 officers. Under NOP, officers, sergeants, and investigators began a process of interacting with neighborhood people for the expressed purpose of identifying and addressing problems of crime and disorder. As a direct result of this interaction, officers were asked to perform multiple functions that ultimately were classified as being reactive, proactive, and coactive in nature. Numerous responsibilities are associated with each of these functions.

The *reactive* function is most commonly associated with the traditional responsibilities of maintaining order and responding to requests for service. Officers were expected to continue to handle calls for service, enforce local and state traffic ordinances, conduct initial investigations, arrest suspects found at crime scenes, and, when visibility was a necessity, perform random, preventive patrol.

The *proactive* function required officers to develop directed or structured patrol strategies in response to various crimes such as burglaries, robberies, street level narcotics, thefts, criminal mischief, etc. occurring within neighborhoods. The purpose of authorizing the use of directed patrols was to initiate action to interdict criminal activity before the situation became worse. As officers learned about criminal activity via crime analysis, they were encouraged to develop tactical plans to address the situation. Included within these plans were a number of strategies, inclusive of, but not limited to the use of: aggressive patrol tactics (e.g., saturation patrols, traffic stops, etc.), covert tactics (e.g., decoys, stakeouts, etc.), and physical surveillance. Where warranted, officers were also empowered to participate in conducting follow-up investigations as a means of interdicting criminal activity.

Despite open debate over the amount of time an officer has available when not handling calls for service, the department encouraged the officers to work with each other and their respective sergeants to proactively redirect their uncommitted time toward specific objectives.

The *coactive* function required officers and the department to actively reach out and systematically work to build relationships with citizens. Officers were allowed to engage in self-direction to become more familiar with their assigned area. It was through self-direction that bonds were formed between officers and citizens who reside and work in the officer's assigned area. The underlying premise of this bond holds that once officers establish contact with citizens, communication will increase. Extensive, consistent communication between citizens and police that focuses on the identification of crime and noncrime problems can lead to a relationship characterized by trust. As trust develops, the willingness to exchange information increases.[3] This is important because, as Skogan notes (1990), citizens hold a virtual monopoly over the information that is the key weapon for combating crime.

In addition to self-direction and developing legitimate working partnerships with citizens, officers were empowered to identify and differentiate strategic crime problems (e.g., narcotics, auto thefts, gang activities, etc.) from tactical ones and develop corresponding strategic plans to address those issues.

Collectively, the reactive, proactive and coactive functions represented a new perspective on delivering services within the community. The utility of this perspective rests on the assumption that the demographic divergence found in cities defies categorical application of a single style of policing. Instead, an officer's role involves the performance of a multiplicity of functions, any of which can be required at any given time, in any given area. Although there may be times when a particular function may be emphasized, this in no way diminishes the importance of the other functions.

This perspective requires involvement of the community through the interactive exchanges between the officers and the citizens. By developing a grassroots process of close interaction, the department's method of establishing goals becomes linked directly to citizen's perceptions and expectations regarding localized needs. Being results-oriented, this perspective places a premium on what is accomplished to improve conditions in the neighborhoods.

Houston managers recognized that the institutionalization of this new perspective required changes in several organizational systems and processes. One of these was the process of performance evaluation. As a result, the decision was made to redesign and test a new performance evaluation process.

Task forces were formed that spent several months articulating the broader role, studying aspects of it in other agencies, exploring a wide range of ideas for documenting and evaluating it, gathering input from other officers, and producing a new performance measurement instrument that reflected their perceptions of their newly conceived roles.

The National Institute of Justice provided funding for an evaluation of the impact on the new process. The study (Wycoff and Oettmeier, 1993a and 1993b) concluded that ". . . a personnel performance measurement process designed to reflect and reinforce the functions that officers are expected to perform can provide structural support for a philosophy of policing and can be a valuable aid in the implementation of organizational change."

The Performance Measurement Workshop

Following the drafting of the research report, the National Institute of Justice supported a workshop, hosted by the Houston Police Department, in which representatives of ten police departments[4] interested in implementing community policing spent three days discussing ways of measuring individual and organizational performance of new roles. Houston's new (and still experimental) performance measurement system and the process of creating it were used as a springboard for discussion. The goal was not to disseminate Houston's product but to use it as a means of provoking response and stimulating additional ideas. The goal was not to produce a model evaluation design within three days; rather, it was to imagine, exchange, and critically examine ideas about alternative approaches. The remainder of this paper shares the workshop discussions with the reader.

The workshop opened the first evening with presentations by the Houston Police Department about what the organization had done to redesign performance measurement and a presentation by the Portland Police Department about what it plans to do as it uses a grant from the National Institute of Justice to reformulate its own performance measurement processes. During the following two and one-half days, the workshop was organized around eight topics:

- Purposes of performance measurement;
- Documenting/measuring what patrol officers do;
- Measuring the effects of officer performance;
- Measuring the performance of investigators and sergeants;
- Measuring the performance of teams;
- Measuring organizational outcomes and the performance of organizational systems;
- Participants in the performance measurement process; and
- Impediments to creating and implementing new performance measurement systems.

During each discussion period, participants divided into two groups, each of which worked with a facilitator to address the same topic. At the end of a discussion period, the groups met to share their work.

Before summarizing workshop deliberations by topic, some general observations about the products of the discussions can be made.

General Observations

Whether it is a source of comfort or despair for the reader, it is the case that participants reached no consensus about ways of measuring individual, team, or agency performance. And this is as it should be, probably *must* be. Even among the small number of agencies represented, there was substantial diversity in the uses made of performance measurement within organizations.

There were those in which performance evaluations affect pay and promotions, and those in which they do not. Some evaluation processes are used to determine disciplinary actions; some are not. Some are used to identify training needs; some are not. Departments varied in whether the nature of their performance evaluation is affected by external constraints (e.g., rules of police and fire commissions, state laws, etc.). Those not shaped by external constraints are open to greater flexibility. Organizations also differ in the historical contexts in which any new performance measurement systems will be created. Some have systems that are less structured and allow greater subjectivity by the evaluator while others have highly structured systems requiring documentation of ratings. Some use numerical scores and some do not. As departments revise their approaches to evaluation, they may want to incorporate some elements of the familiar system (unless loathing of it is great) for the sake of increasing acceptance of the new process.

All these variables suggest that performance measurement, like community policing itself, needs to be tailored to the characteristics of the agency and the community it serves. Despite problems encountered or principles advocated, the process of measuring performance must be flexible enough to capture the broad spectrum and diversity of accomplishments. It was for this reason the topics of the workshop were designed to have broad applicability.

Purposes of Performance Measurement

What is measured and how it is measured should depend on the reasons for collecting the data. Mastrofski and Wadman (1991) identify three principal reasons for measuring employee performance:

> ***Administration:*** to help managers make decisions about promotion, demotion, reward, discipline, training needs, salary, job assignment, retention, and termination.

Guidance and Counseling: to help supervisors provide feedback to subordinates and assist them in career planning and preparation, and to improve employee motivation.

Research: to validate selection and screening tests and training evaluations and to assess the effectiveness of interventions designed to improve individual performances.

To these three reasons, the Houston Police Department, in the course of conducting its performance measurement project, added three more:

Socialization: to convey expectations to personnel about both the content and the style of their performance, to reinforce other means of organizational communication about the mission and values of the department.

Documentation: to record the types of problems and situations officers are addressing in their neighborhoods and the approaches they take to them. Such documentation provides for data-based analysis of the types of resources and other managerial support needed to address the problems and allows officers the opportunity to have their efforts recognized.

System Improvement: to identify organizational conditions that may impede improved performance and to solicit ideas for changing the conditions.

Participants in the workshop identified among themselves several purposes for which their organizations evaluate the performance of individual officers. These included:

- influencing promotions or transfer to special assignments;
- determining raises or merit pay;
- identifying training needs of the officers;
- identifying ways to improve performance of individual officers;
- documenting and planning an officer's career development;

- establishing documentation that might be needed in disciplinary hearings; and

- communicating role expectations to the officer.

Most participants identified only one or two of these purposes as characterizing performance measurement in their own agencies, and at least one could identify no use made of current personnel evaluations currently are put. The diversity of possible uses was acknowledged, and it was agreed that managers would need to establish the primary purposes of performance measurement before new processes and criteria were designed.

One issue of critical importance to managers is establishing consensus within and between ranks about the purpose of performance measurement. In many instances, not only are there differing opinions among sergeants, but also among lieutenants about how and on what criteria officers should be assessed. In both cases, the collective agreement among sergeants and lieutenants may be in conflict with what the officers advocate as being important, especially given the familiarity officers may have with neighborhood service delivery demands. These potential differences must be clarified and resolved so any new processes and criteria will match their intended purposes.

Documenting/Measuring What Patrol Officers Do

The participants spent considerable time attempting to answer two questions: What should be measured? How should it be measured?

What should be measured? Participants agreed, to some extent, the that the answer should depend on what needs to be done in the area where the officer works. The focus should center on activities and/or accomplishments.

Documenting activities could lead to substantial noncomparability of evaluations across officers and even for the same officer over time, since what needs to be done could vary by area and within one area over time.

This variation, coupled with the frequency of performing the activities, directly affects the opportunity for the officer to be evaluated. The more activities performed, the higher the probability an officer will be observed by the sergeant and graded accordingly.

Commonly used evaluation criteria are not very useful for assessing activities and accomplishments. Traditional performance measurement emphasizes an officer's knowledge, skills and abilities (KSAs). Although assessing KSAs should not be minimized in terms of providing officers information that is valuable to their self development, this type of assessment tells us very little about what is being done to address crime and disorder issues within a neighborhood. In other words, the net affect of performance evaluations has been to improve the officer and not the neighborhood.

To correct this deficiency, performance criteria should be expanded to incorporate the documentation of activities and processes that are crucial to determining the effectiveness of results attained over time.

Using broader based or different types of evaluation categories was suggested so sergeants could determine whether an officer was attempting to identify what needed to be done and was attempting to respond to specific problems in an area. This kind of "opinion" on the part of the sergeant might be more subjective than some measures now in use, but participants tended to believe the judgment could be more useful than some "hard" data currently collected by some agencies.

This type of evaluation requires a sergeant to be well informed about the officer's efforts. Herein lies another potential problem. If sergeants are expected to spend more time observing and meeting with officers, some will feel they do not have enough time to do everything expected of them. If this is the case, priorities will have to be established regarding the responsibilities of the sergeants. Failure to do this may result in the sergeants ultimately rejecting the new performance measurement process.

The idea of documenting, even counting, some kinds of behaviors was not rejected by the group. An argument was made that officers should be able to discuss (and that sergeants should expect them to discuss) their *reasons* for performing the activities that produced the number(s). An activity should not be repeated or reinforced simply for the sake of the activity itself (e.g., we do it because it has always been done). The results of an activity should be analyzed to determine if they were consistent with expected outcomes for the service demand in question. Serendipitous findings should be expected and analyzed as well.

Participants also recognized that in policing, as in many other service professions, it is not only what you do that counts; the way in which you perform a particular activity may be equally as important. Discussions dealt with the importance of incorporating "style" as a performance criterion for officers (e.g., Is the officer perceived as friendly, concerned, willing, helpful, etc. by persons receiving the service?).

How should performance be measured? There was consensus that evaluation in the context of community policing would require a close relationship between the officer and the immediate sergeant. The nature of this relationship is dependent upon a the sergeant's span of control and workload.

Traditional spans of control (e.g., 1 sergeant to 8 or 10 officers) will need to be reduced. It may be necessary to re-examine the sergeant's role to determine whether all its traditional functions do need to be performed and whether some can be delegated to other persons.

The community policing sergeant would need to be familiar with the area the officer works, the problems and concerns within that area, and the efforts made by the officer to address those issues. Considerable knowledge would most effectively be derived from frequent conversations between the officer and sergeant. These discussions could be guided by using weekly or monthly assessment forms that target specific problems, activities, and expected results.

The sergeant would need to have more information than the officer's view about problems and activities. The discussion groups suggested several means of acquiring information about officer performance:

- direct entry of information by other sergeants into a computer using a predefined software format;
- maintaining a "log" of observations about officer recommendations, accomplishments, and failures ascertained from frequent coaching sessions between the officer and sergeant;
- input from the "community" that could be obtained through:
  - direct communication between the sergeant and community representatives;
  - citizen letters directed to the officer, sergeant, division commander, or Chief of Police;
  - survey responses from service recipients; comments from citizens attending community meetings; and
  - news stories.
- verbal or written communication with other agencies (e.g., sheriff department's, courts, probation/parole officers, social service agency representatives, etc.), inclusive of other city departments and private sector organizations; and
- an officer "resume" in which the officer periodically would report career progress and significant events or activities of which the officer would want the sergeant and organization to be aware. The resume could include information about education and training that could be used by the department to determine special, temporary or permanent assignments.

Measuring the Effects of Officer Performance

This was a more difficult topic since most departments are not in the business of measuring the effects, outcomes, or impacts of officers' efforts. Traditional management postures have required officers to emphasize means over ends. For example, traffic enforcement typically is measured in terms of the number of tickets issued for moving violations (e.g., improper turns, running red lights, speeding, etc.). The association seldom is made between the need to issue speeding tickets and the need to reduce minor accidents or fatalities at a particular location. Police managers are only beginning to address the need to evaluate performance in relation to specific problems.

According to Goldstein (1990), evaluating police response to any problem requires the following:

- a clear understanding of the problem;
- agreement over the specific interest(s) to be served in dealing with the problem, and their order of importance;
- agreement on the method to be used to determine the extent to which these interests (or goals) are reached;
- a realistic assessment of what might be expected of the police (e.g., solving the problem versus improving the quality of the police management of it);
- determination of the relative importance of short-term versus long-term impact; and
- a clear understanding of the legality and fairness of the response (recognizing that reducing a problem through improper use of authority is not only wrong, but likely to be counterproductive because of its effects on other aspects of police operations).

Goldstein (1990) cautions against defining success as problem eradication since many problems by their very nature are intractable or unmanageable because of their magnitude. Despite this limitation, there are a sufficient number of problems well within the boundaries of police control that merit attention.

In struggling with the meaning of "effectiveness" as it pertains to problem-oriented policing, Spelman and Eck (1987) have developed five varying degrees of impact the police may have on a problem. They encompass:

- total elimination;
- reducing the number of incidents it creates;
- reducing the seriousness of the incidents it creates;
- designing methods for better handling the incidents; and
- removing the problems from police consideration (assuming it is dealt with more effectively by some other entity than the police).

In this context, Goldstein (1990) claims that for much of police business, the most realistic goal is to reduce the number of incidents that a problem creates and to reduce the seriousness of these incidents. Correspondingly, he suggests it is helpful to characterize the police role more realistically as "managing deviance" and then concentrate on equipping the police to carry out this management role with greater effectiveness. It is highly unlikely that many departments today have evolved to a point where individual or organizational performances are gauged in this manner. But, despite the difficulty of doing so, it is an important goal for community policing agencies.

The workshop participants agreed that outcomes to be measured should be directly related to the goals of the department. Yet these goals can be quite diverse depending upon the organization's orientation. Some departments emphasize goals related to specific community-wide issues. Examples would include:

(1) handling DWIs/DUIs;

(2) handling domestic violence cases;

(3) reducing gang activities;

(4) responding to narcotic/illegal prescription drug activities;

(5) addressing early release for parolees;

(6) lowering response times;

(7) reducing crime rates, etc. In each of these instances, the police have the option of involving the community as they seek to address the issue in question.

Other agencies today establish goals that require citizen participation at local levels. These include, but are not limited to: reducing fear among citizens, increasing citizen satisfaction with the police, increasing the ability of the community to address certain types of problems, reducing victimization rates, etc. Indications of success for some of these goals can be obtained from responses to community surveys.

And finally, some departments seek to establish goals that reflect different expectations existing within neighborhoods. This perspective is the most challenging because it requires management to allocate resources on the basis of competing demands. It is far easier to deploy personnel solely on the basis of lowering response times than it is to address different types of tactical or strategic crime problems while maintaining an acceptable range of response times.

Objective outcome measures do exist for some neighborhood problems. If, for example, the goal of a particular strategy were to reduce repeat calls to a residence experiencing recurring domestic disturbances, it would be simple enough to document the calls to the address over time from computer reports. Efforts to reduce vandalism might be gauged by the number of graffiti sites, number of broken street lights, number of defaced traffic signs, etc. While these numbers may indicate a lack of activity in an area, one should not necessarily conclude the reasons for the vandalism have been addressed.

Workshop participants agreed that measurement of problem solving effectiveness should not be used to "grade" the officer. It was argued that "grading," insofar as it is done, should be based on effort rather than effect. Officers should be able to identify the measurable conditions they would expect to see change before they undertake a problem solving effort. They should also be allowed to identify factors that can affect outcomes not under an officer's or organization's control.

Measuring the Performance of Investigators

Most of the attention over the past few years with community policing has focused on the patrol officer. There has been less written about the investigative function in the community policing context. The most frequent recommendation is that the function be decentralized.

The primary reason for decentralization is to assign investigators to a neighborhood(s) in which they would become crime generalists and area specialists. Decentralized investigators would be responsible for neighborhood investigations.

Centralized investigators would be responsible for conducting specific citywide investigations. Hence, they would be crime specialists and area generalists. Centralized investigators would continue to remain experts for a single type of crime on a citywide basis while decentralized investigators would become experts about crime within their respective neighborhoods.[5]

Despite these apparent differences, the work of centralized and decentralized investigators is reciprocal; there is a degree of mutual dependency in the performance of their work. Furthermore, under the auspices of community policing, integration must occur between the patrol and investigative functions. This will require the sharing of information between and among patrol officers and investigators. It will also require a commitment on behalf of patrol and investigative personnel to assume a sense of shared responsibility for the delivery of police services.

This sense of "shared responsibility" has a significant effect on the nature of performance criteria for decentralized investigative personnel. According to the participants, investigators are generally assessed using any number of criteria, such as: proper execution of search warrants, use of informants, taking accurate statements, courtroom testimony, evidence collection, case management, and clearance rates (informal). Under the context of community policing, these criteria do not become any less important. Rather, there is the potential for broadening the scope of emphasis.

As investigators move toward becoming generalists assigned to specific areas, responsibilities begin to evolve as well. These changes include, but are not limited to:

- familiarity with assigned area;
- the type of interaction with patrol officers, operational support personnel and citizens;
- expanded investigative skills (reflecting the generalists nature of their assignment);
- problem solving ability;
- contributing in the development of training criteria that will support patrol operations, the management of criminal investigation, and the quality of the interaction with the public;
- participation in the development and implementation of crime prevention strategies; and
- commitment to teamwork which will facilitate functional interaction with patrol personnel.

Agencies working under the context of community policing should be working to develop new performance criteria for investigators based on these responsibilities.

Measuring the Performance of Sergeants

Sergeants perform a variety of roles, the most prevalent of which include:

- Administrative: coping with the day-to-day paperwork demands, securing compliance with standard operating procedures, authorizing days off, vacation, etc.;

- Interpersonal communications: interacting with personnel to help resolve problems, answer questions, provide advice, knowing when to listen and when to converse; and

- Career development: authorizing officers to attend training, encouraging them to attend school, assisting them in their promotional endeavors, explore work and academic interests, etc.

The most important role, however, is the *managerial* one. This role, more than any other, is critical to the performance of officers under community policing. As managers, sergeants must be able to collect data, analyze it to identify problems, and either respond efficiently or coordinate efficient responses to those problems. The sergeants must be independent thinkers, who thrive on creativity and innovation. They must pride themselves on self-initiation and self-direction. They must strive to work with their officers to obtain qualitative results.

Qualitative results will be a product of the sergeant's efforts plus the synergism obtained from working with the support systems within the organization and community. This will require sergeants to perform more as coaches, advisors, facilitators, and coordinators than task masters. Since a community based department will operate as an open system, the sergeants will be required to develop and maintain a community perspective as it relates to their areas of responsibility. This means sergeants will assume responsibility for working with community resources within their sphere of influence and control to improve neighborhood conditions. Understanding cultural diversity within the community and learning how to incorporate differing suggestions will become a valued skill for sergeants and not a liability to be given little attention.

In this context, workshop participants strongly supported developing performance criteria from the following considerations:

- communication with patrol officers about strategic and tactical responses to neighborhood crime and disorder problems;

- interaction with community leaders to develop a global perspective of needs and demands;

- leadership qualities appropriate to the assigned area;

- participation in/support for problem solving at the neighborhood level;

- knowledge of what officers need (including system changes) in order to accomplish job(s);

- coordination of officers' efforts across multiple assignments;

- monitoring the "appropriateness" of officers' relationship with community representatives;

- familiarity with what officers have done, are doing, and would like to do; and

- ability to encourage the development of new skills within their officers.

The importance of these managerial considerations cannot be overstated. If functional responsibilities from evolving roles are to be integrated within the organization, managerial styles and practices must change accordingly.

Measuring the Performance of Teams

Some organizational plans for community policing call for the configuration of employees into teams that provide service to areas of the community; other plans do not rely on teams. Workshop participants were divided on the question of whether their own organizations were likely to need performance measures designed to reflect the work of teams but all worked to develop the following team performance criteria:

- ability of the group to work together (e.g., cohesiveness, unity, shared purpose, etc.);

- the effective use of individual skills;

- competence in addressing community issues, ranging from the performance of daily tasks to complex projects;

- ability to engage the citizenry, other city departments, community groups, etc., in addressing local problems;

- adaptability or flexibility to change;
- ability of a team to function as a part of the organization;
- ability to identify community problems and reach a consensus on method(s) to define solution(s); and
- outcomes produced by teams.

Independent of the service philosophies, most departments do make use of some organized teams, whether they are S.W.A.T. teams, dive teams, bomb squads, gang squads, or other types of tactical groups. Typically, these groups are not evaluated as teams, and workshop participants suggested that some of the criteria they have developed for community policing teams could be modified for application to these tactical teams.

There is another sense in which every department makes use of "teams" if one considers that there are ad hoc "incident teams" that form and reform several times a day in most agencies. Such "teams" consist of the people in the organization whose actions are focused on dealing with the same incident, even though some of the "team" members might not have direct contact with each other. For each incident of assault that occurs, there is an assault incident team that might include:

- call taker/dispatcher;
- responding officers;
- crime scene technician (if necessary);
- investigator;
- records clerk; and
- victim advocate.

If the department used a survey to measure citizen satisfaction with police response to assaults and other incidents, it typically would be designed to reflect the erroneous assumption that the behavior of the responding officers is the only or primary determinant of citizen attitudes. However, if the survey took into account the responses of all police participants involved in the case(s), an analysis could reveal any number of areas for improvements. Accordingly, with appropriate training and feedback to affected employees, a comprehensive approach toward improving the quality of customer service can be instituted. In this respect, the individuals might become more inclined to behave in a "team-like" manner despite belonging to independent work units within the organization.

Measuring Organizational Outcomes and the Performance of Organizational Systems

According to Mastrofski and Wadman (1991), performance measurement has two fundamental components: (1) defining what police ought to accomplish (the normative perspective) and (2) defining what they can accomplish or have accomplished (the empirical perspective). In determining what police ought to accomplish, performance measures are usually grouped according to effectiveness, efficiency, equity, and accountability. The measures derived from these factors are generally quantifiable in nature and thereby are very attractive to police executives. The trade-offs among these factors (discussed earlier in this article) also help to determine which performance measures an agency will pursue. These are important performance measures regardless of the organization's philosophical commitment.

Determining what a police organization *can* accomplish is more difficult to ascertain because no one can say with certainty what is attainable. Historically, police departments have maintained they are fully capable of determining what they can and should accomplish with regard to providing police services. However, with the advent of community policing, police executives are discovering that officers and citizens can provide more accurate information about service demands and a more in-depth understanding of community issues and how to deal with them than they ever thought was possible.

There are at least two ways in which community input can be incorporated into an agency's decisionmaking. (1) It can be solicited and combined with internally generated input as a means of shaping decisions regarding global service delivery commitments. (2) Community input at the neighborhood level can be used to help prioritize police responses within an area for a given time period. This form of "power sharing" is predicated to some extent on the neighborhood's resolve to contribute resources or otherwise assist the police in addressing the identified problems or concerns.

As decisions are made regarding the allocation of resources to address problems, community input can also be used to help identify expected outcomes. This is useful for three reasons. First, citizens quickly learn what the police can and cannot accomplish given the problem in question and the availability of resources. Second, citizens will feel ownership in forming a coactive partnership with the police. They will be more apt to follow through with their commitments. Third, the synergism generated from the interaction may result in identifying problem resolution strategies not normally expected. As desirable as these outcomes are, incorporating citizen input into the decision-making process, especially as it pertains to identifying performance criteria, is difficult to accomplish.

This responsibility should not be placed on the shoulders of operations personnel and their immediate superiors. Executives need to assume responsibility for constructing management systems within the organization which will incorporate citizen input as a means of facilitating goal attainment. These systems should not be limited to patrol and investigative operations. Citizen input can be constructive in other areas as well (e.g., personnel behavior, training and education, call intake/dispatch operations, etc.).

In many, if not most, departments, segments within the organization that, at least in theory, are considered to be support divisions, have come to operate separately, serving their own ends as much as the larger goals of the agency. In few organizations, for example, are the investigative functions and the communications functions organized to work in conjunction with patrol operations. They work independently. Therefore, performance measures for these divisions or groups may reflect their internal goals rather than the goals of the organization. Attention may be directed toward compliance with procedures to ensure administrative efficiency (e.g., processing cases, adhering to legal procedures, writing reports, conducting expedient investigations, etc.).

While these may be appropriate, there also should be performance measures that indicate whether the work that is done produces desired results. Compliance with procedures should be linked to results and divisions, like the organization, should be results-oriented.

The challenge for executives is to create division objectives that are compatible with organizational goals. Toward this end, workshop participants suggested that an organization assess itself and its separate divisions in terms of whether the right things are being done rather than only in terms of whether things are being done correctly.

"Support" was a key concept in the discussions. Participants suggested that criteria for agency performance need to be established that reflect the agency's support of both it employees and the citizens. There was strong sentiment that officers should be involved in helping establish both sets of criteria. It was suggested that departments regularly conduct employee personnel surveys to determine what employees think about how the agency and its various divisions are performing.

There was some discussion of whether the accreditation process was a performance measure by which agencies should be held accountable. There was general agreement the accreditation process can help determine an agency's capacity for managing service. It does not, however, provide a guide as to what the service should include, nor is it capable of measuring the quality of the service delivered. It is up to the agency, working with the community, to establish criteria for service delivery.

Participants recommended that organizational managers use periodic community surveys, and review sessions with formal and informal community leaders and the media to assess organizational performance, or, at least perceptions of organizational performance in the community. "Review sessions" could be focused on questions as open and general as: "How do you think we are doing?" and "What are the areas you think we need to work on?" The request for this kind of review should be initiated by police executives. The discussants agreed many that police managers initially might feel uncomfortable with this kind of public discussion of organizational performance. Even though the first session or two might be somewhat awkward, it was felt that as the "reviews" were repeated, a greater sense of trust and contribution could develop among participants, and the community would have an increased sense of the agency being open and accessible to the public.

Participants in the Performance Measurement Process

Traditionally, individual performance evaluations have been conducted by an employee's immediate superior.

Given the inability of the superior to verify everything on which a person could and should be assessed, feedback from other sources is an option. Workshop participants suggested that individual performance assessments incorporate feedback from other officers, their immediate superior, other managers, investigators, service recipients, appropriate community representatives and representatives from other agencies, city departments or private sector service agencies. Team and organization evaluations could utilize the same sources as well as feedback from the media.

Impediments to Creating and Implementing New Performance Measurement Systems

This topic was designed to allow participants to share concerns and experiences about the process of developing new performance measurement, both in general and as it relates specifically to community policing.

With respect to evaluating impacts of community policing, the major concern shared by the group was that efforts to evaluate effectiveness would be premature. The redirection of an organization is a long-term undertaking that cannot be rushed for the sake of attempting to meet what may be unrealistic expectations. Efforts to evaluate departments that are in the process of becoming community based organizations initially should be limited to process evaluations. This form of assessment is capable of measuring steps taken to convert the organization from one service approach to another.

In commenting on the design of individual performance evaluations, participants discussed their concern about acquiring enough input from line officers without getting "too much" information. The participants realized there are multiple purposes for, and perspectives about, performance evaluation; while officer input is essential, other personnel also ought to have a say about redesigning instrumentation. Sergeants, for example, usually will have the primary responsibility for administering any new performance evaluation process. If they are not included in the design process, the changes will not benefit from the experience of sergeants, and they may not readily accept the new approach.

Workshop participants were concerned about employee acceptance of any new process or instrumentation and discussed possible opposition by unions or by civil service commissions. In response to this issue, the discussion focused again on the importance of including all "stakeholders" in the design process.

Related to this was the point that the new measurement methods should not be so radically different from the old ones that they are rejected on that basis alone. The suggestion was made that revision of performance measurement should be a common practice in an organization—not something done once every twenty or forty years. Just as the job should keep changing to reflect the needs of the community and increasing professional knowledge, so should the measurement process be modified frequently to reflect the nature of the job. If revised frequently, methods of performance measurement should need only minor modification rather than radical revision, and the change will be less jarring to the organization.

Participants explored the issue of fairness of evaluations in a community policing context. How could an officer assigned to an area with few problems be equitably compared to an officer assigned to an area with numerous grave problems? Perhaps each officer should be judged on the basis of a performance "contract" that reflects the conditions of the neighborhood and the availability of the officer and resources to provide a greater range of services.

A similar issue was raised about the evaluation of the same officer who worked across time in the same area. As the officer succeeded in improving conditions in the community, there would be fewer problems to address. If performance measurement was based, at least in part, on the problem solving efforts of the officer, how would the supervisor distinguish between an officer who had been a successful problem solver and one who simply had grown lazy over time? It was suggested these types of questions reinforce the need for measures of effectiveness of problem solving efforts. Performance measurement should capture both effort and outcome.

The issue of complexity of performance evaluation systems was discussed, and the argument was made for simplicity—for not trying to collect more information than reasonably could be expected to be used. Sergeants should not feel overwhelmed by the task of evaluation. A good process, however simple or detailed, should leave both the officer and sergeant feeling the sergeant is well informed about the officer's work and working conditions.

Finally, the group reminded itself that under the best conditions, the evaluation process can be stressful and potentially painful. Even in agencies where evaluations are viewed as "not counting for anything," officers can react with considerable passion to the change of a few points in their evaluations from one period to the next. Concern for the welfare of the employee, as well as attention to management and organizational issues, should guide the design of the evaluation process.

Conclusion

The workshop produced no simple answers to the issues of performance measurement. Nor did participants think there is a single model that would apply across agencies over time.

A community policing philosophy suggests a model of performance evaluation that reflects the needs of both the officer (and organization) and the needs of the community or neighborhood in which the officer works. Traditionally, even the best performance evaluations have been used only to monitor officer performance and provide constructive feedback to the individual. The development of the officer should continue to be an important goal of performance assessment, but, under community policing, the continuing development of an experienced officer would be tied to the welfare of the neighborhood. The areas of an officer's skill base that would be marked for improvement would be those necessary to improve the quality of services needed in the neighborhood. In this way, performance measurement becomes a means to the end of improving neighborhood safety.

This perspective illustrates the importance of having executives commit personnel to regular reviews of the organization's performance evaluation system to ensure both the citizens and the employees are served properly. By anchoring performance measurement to the community, a dynamic process will be established. As an area improves or deteriorates, police and citizens can make corresponding adjustments to measurement criteria. In this way, the revision of performance measurement will help employees remain aware that their job is that of serving the community.

Notes

The authors are deeply indebted to the participants of the Performance Measurement Workshop. Their involvement in the workshop provided valuable insights, observations and ideas.

[1] The record of researchers is no better in this respect than the record of police managers. Despite their disclaimers about the validity and reliability of such indicators, researchers continue to use recorded

crime data, arrest data and administrative data as indicators of performance and outcome because other indicators are unavailable or are too costly or time-consuming to create. This fact led to Kelling's (1978) call for "... a modest moratorium on the application of crime related productivity measures" until the full range of the police role could be documented and decisions made about how to measure a much wider range of police activity.

[2] Discretion and the greater flexibility it gives an officer for how, when and where to use time is not a new issue for supervisors. It has always been an issue for rural police departments and sheriff's agencies in which officers and supervisors may never have occasion to meet after roll call (and, sometimes, not even at roll call). Researchers need to develop information about supervision in these types of agencies.

[3] The formula of Contact-Communication-Trust-Information Exchange was developed by former Houston Police Department Lieutenant David Sitz as part of the orientation training officers received prior to actually experimenting with the implementation of their new responsibilities.

[4] Participating agencies included police departments from Austin, Texas; Boulder, Colorado; Houston, Texas; Minneapolis, Minnesota; Newport News, Virginia; Portland, Oregon; St. Louis, Missouri; St. Petersburg, Florida; Spokane, Washington; and the Sheriff's Office of Green County, South Carolina. The University of Oregon, National Institute of Justice and Police Foundation also were represented.

[5] For a more comprehensive discussion of this issue, see: Integrating Investigative Operations Through Neighborhood Oriented Policing, by T.N. Oettmeier and W.H. Bieck, Houston Police Department, 1987.

References

Bittner, E. (1972). *The Functions of the Police in Modern Society.* Rockville, MD.: National Institute of Mental Health.

Dallas Police Department (1972). *Five Year Plan.* Dallas, TX: Dallas Police Department.

Gabor, A. (1991). "Take This Job and Love It." *New York Times,* January 26.

Goldstein, H. (1979). "Improving Policing: A Problem Oriented Approach." *Crime and Delinquency,* 25.

Goldstein, H. (1990). *Problem Oriented Policing.* New York, NY: McGraw Hill Publishing.

Kelling, G. and M. Moore (1988). *The Evolving Strategy of Policing.* Washington, D.C.: National Institute of Justice

Kelling, G. (1992). "Measuring What Matters: A New Way of Thinking About Crime and Public Order." *The City Journal.* Spring.

Mastrofski, S. and R. Wadman (1991). "Personnel and Agency Performance Measurement." In W. Geller (ed.), *Local Government Police Management.* Washington, D.C.: International City Managers Association.

Sherman, L. (1973). *Team Policing.* Washington, D.C.: National Institute of Justice.

Spellman, W. and J. Eck (1987). "Newport News Tests Problem Oriented Policing." Washington, D.C.: National Institute of Justice.

Weisburd, D., J. McElroy, and P. Hardyman (1989). "Maintaining Control in Community-Oriented Policing." In D. Kenney (ed.), *Police and Policing: Contemporary Issues.* New York, NY: Praeger.

Wycoff, M. (1982). " Improving Police Performance Measurement: One More Voice." *The Urban Interest.* Spring, 1982, 8-16.

Wycoff, M. (1982b). *The Role of Municipal Police: Research as Prelude to Changing It.* Washington, D.C.: Police Foundation.

Wycoff, M. and T. Oettmeier (1993a). "Evaluating Patrol Officer Performance Under Community Policing: The Houston Experience." Washington, D.C.: National Institute of Justice.

Wycoff, M. and T. Oettmeier (1993b). "Evaluating Patrol Officer Performance Under Community Policing: The Houston Experience." Washington, D.C.: National Institute of Justice.

Political Obligation: Connecting Police Ethics and Democratic Values

Philip W. Rhoades
Corpus Christi State University

I am not satisfied that our pursuit of law enforcement ethics is proceeding on an appropriate track, in consideration of "professional ethics" as applied to traditional professions. We may have moved too quickly to this form of applied ethics prior to establishing its appropriateness for the police occupation. My concern stems from the need to provide a foundation for police ethics in the fundamental values of democratic society and the nature of public service.

This concern arises because the model chosen for an analytical framework limits the values chosen for examination and the way the individual is led to view personal obligations and responsibilities. Sherman (1981:43) points out that our effort to teach and learn about ethics "requires an analysis of both relevant facts and values within a coherent ethical framework of principles and premises." In the search for an appropriate framework, the police appear to be embracing concepts and practices developed in the traditional professions. With some ambivalence, the police appear to believe in professionalism (Price, 1977:93-94) and some form of the professional model. The occupation is described as engaged in a gradual evolution toward one which has the characteristics of a profession (Price, 1977; More, 1985:303-311; Walker, 1983:243-246; Broderick, 1987:233-234). Within the professional model appear the concepts of a service ethic (More, 1985:310), the need to clarify the profession-society relationship (Price, 1977:98), the problem of professional autonomy (Broderick, 1987:234-236; Walker, 1983:245), and the need for a code of ethics (Johnson & Copus, 1981). Attempts to develop these have led to the borrowing of aspects of applied ethics as practiced in the traditional professions such as law and medicine (Heffernan, 1982; Sherman, 1981, 1982; Johnson & Copus, 1981; Pollock-Byrne, 1989; Delattre, 1989; Delaney, 1990; Metz, 1990).

However, Sherman (1981:43) warns that not all frameworks for the analysis of ethical issues are appropriate for application to criminal justice and, more narrowly, law enforcement. Elliston and Bowie (1982:xi) note the application of some current frameworks may require them to be "reworked, redesigned, and occasionally overhauled to yield their insights." These warnings should be taken seriously, because the application of traditional professional ethics may lead to analytical frameworks and value choices that create ethical dilemmas rather than assist in their solution. The professional ethics framework conceals the true nature of the police occupation's clientele, provides for the adoption of too much autonomy, leads to inappropriate prioritization of values, and results in assumption of discretion that is insufficiently limited. Even with redesign, traditional frameworks for professional ethics cannot be adequate for policing.

We need an analytical framework for applied ethics that leads the police directly to a consideration of facts and values relevant to their responsibilities as public servants in a democratic society. For the police, values for analysis within their applied ethics should come not from self definition of the profession, nor from a service ethic that delimits professional-client relations, but from the inherent nature of the occupation.

Like Tussman (1970:15), I believe we should direct effort

> toward a theory of political obligation—an attempt at the delineation of the demands of the political role and of propriety in response to those demands, obligations, or duties. A theory of political obligation is an attempt to provide the elements of an answer to the political agent's "What should I do?"

The police should be viewed, not as traditional professionals, but as public agents within representative bureaucracies with clear political obligations. This would bind them more fully to democratic values than professional ethics and would provide justification from those democratic values of several developments in policing.

Public Purpose and Democratic Values

It is assumed that public bureaucracies in a democracy ought to find their operating principles from among the values widely held, especially those that are fundamental in this society. The police are viewed here as Goldstein (1977:33) recommends, predominantly as agencies of local government. As such, they have an inherently public purpose, although debate remains as to how to describe that purpose.

The correctness of decisions made and actions taken by police officers is directly tied to whether they contribute to or restrain the reaching of organizational purpose and ultimately the values which that purpose is established to serve. The "notion of purpose intrinsically contains some measure of value linked to an implied ethical mandate. . . . Purpose implies value, and value in action is ethics" (Gawthrop, 1984:7). This is so because "the distinction between right and wrong is inherent in action . . . . All action is valuation" (Wren, 1974). For the public administrator, then,

> [i]ndividual ethical behavior is possible only to the extent that it is linked directly to a supportive value structure that, in turn, introduces a sense of direction and purposefulness into the decision-making processes of public organizations (Gawthrop, 1984:36).

This principle links the police directly with democratic values because it is these values that the society was formed to foster and that form the basis for the purpose of the police institution. It ties the police with these values in the development of ethics and moral codes.

> It seems to me that the strongest argument to be made for governmental ethical behavior is one that derives from the purpose of the institution: the business of government is the business of protecting and preserving those conditions generally believed necessary for the continuance of a civil association in which individuals can lead lives they regard as worthwhile. The preservation of that civil environment also may be the very reason morality was invented. Hence, there is a commonality of purpose in the invention of morality and of government. Any other use of governmental office is a perversion of office (French, 1983:12).

Thus, an identity of purpose is found between the values that underlie the reason for government, for police systems, and for social norms. Therefore, police ethics should be formulated from these values and the principles that may be generated from them.

Democratic Values Can Be Identified

To move forward in the development of police ethics, the description and analysis of the democratic values that create that foundation becomes work of great importance. These values are the political and social values that are inherent within this society's form of representative democracy. These may include, but are not limited to, a general belief in consent of the governed, general majority rule with sincere protection of minority and individual interests, the avoidance of tyranny, openness in government administration, equal opportunity to engage in politics, and the expectation of citizen participation.

Both as a reason for and a result of this form of government, substantive values of freedom, life, property, privacy, and welfare are to be preserved and enhanced by government action (Bayles, 1981:6). Also, procedural values such as the rule of law, due process, equal protection, presumption of innocence, propriety, freedom from cruel and unusual punishment, and fairness are part of this foundation (Newman & Anderson, 1989).

Description and analysis of this foundation are critical, but have not been sufficiently emphasized in policing. Extensive guides exist for this work in politics and public administration. It is in this analysis that we will confront competing or conflicting values and gain a sense of value priorities in policing.

The society's fundamental documents should be examined as one source of these values and value conflicts. "The Constitution, then, which is the process by which governmental action is effectively restrained, *functions* also as the most effective symbol of the unifying forces operative in a community" (Friedrich, 1968:170). Indeed, Goldstein (1977:12-14) argues that the police should form a commitment to "preserving and extending democratic values" as their primary goal. He finds their obligations not just to be the exercise of "their limited authority in conformity with the Constitution" but in seeing "to it that others do not infringe on constitutionally guaranteed rights." Thus, such documents and analysis of them become fundamental parts of ethical inquiry for the police.

Additional assistance in discovery of democratic values may be found from those who comment upon the American scene. Myrdal (1962:4) provides us with one useful point of departure. He argues that the

> ideals of the essential dignity of the individual human being, of the fundamental equality of all men, and of certain inalienable rights to freedom, justice, and a fair opportunity represent to the American people the essential meaning of the nation's early struggle for independence.

Many such analyses of the evolving values of our society exist for us to examine. Once some consensus is found on broad value concepts we can generate specific principles to assist in the development of police ethics.

Efforts to derive specific principles have begun. Schmalleger and Gustafson (1981:4) indicate that fairness, harmony, and order are values that the criminal justice system needs to operationalize. Gustafson (1981:293-300) derives the following value assumptions from an exercise in this process of operationalization:

1. Citizens are responsible for their community;

2. When disrupted the community must be restored;

3. The criminal justice system must be sensitive to the need for its procedures to be consistent with the facts;

4. Respect for all persons and equal treatment of all persons must prevail;

5. The presumption of innocence must be safeguarded in the system;

6. Protection of the poor, weak, and unpopular must be recognized; and

7. The community must recognize the rights of victims.

From this example, one can conclude that derivation of guiding principles from basic democratic values is possible.

What I seek to describe is a connection between these values and police ethics that is more compelling than the connection found in professional ethics. We need to find analytical frameworks that encourage a much closer, frequent, and extensive examination of fundamental democratic values than professional ethics require. A framework is needed that will provide a tool for the application of moral arguments to answer practical questions and assist in teaching and learning about the values, duties, and virtues one ought to have in the public service (Lilla, 1981:11-15). This framework should not only permit us to study "moral questions, or the means for deciding about which is right or wrong and what ought to be done in particular situations," but it also ought to assist us in making choices about metaethics, "or the study of the concepts and terms that underlie reasoning about morals" (Sherman 1982:14). This framework can be found in the consideration of political obligation and by seeing police agencies as representative bureaucracies.

Professional Ethics are Inadequate

In binding professional ethics to the values of the society, professional ethics appear flawed for application to the police. Professional ethics attempt to bind one to values found in one's self interests, profession, and society. However, the latter bond is a weak, optional, and lower-order obligation, unlike that necessary for policing.

Camenish (1983:96-97) states that the professional is a citizen of the society and the profession forms a subcommunity. The "nature and function of the subcommunity . . . . reflect and depend upon important elements in the larger society-its needs and the needs of its members, its dominant values, etc." (Camenish, 1983:98). Bayles (1981:5) states that "[o]nly against an understanding of the values of liberal society and the general role of professions can the peculiarities of ethical issues confronting the different professions be properly analyzed and perhaps resolved." Yet after such analysis, professional ethics provide only weak and perhaps optional commitment to democratic values. The professional is obligated to democratic values only through the role of citizen, and as may be required to maintain the unique, separate role of the profession. Neither of these moral connections is as strong as that required of the police.

For professions, the moral connections and obligations seen by Camenish (1983:99-109) come from promises made by the professionals, roles, and therefore, role expectations accepted, and gifts received that entail obligations. All of these permit discretion in their application and considerable interpretation by the professional. Bayles (1981:19) provides a statement of professional obligation which demonstrates this point.

> Professional activity should promote the wealth of the professionals and the interests of the clients related to the professional function (such as legal justice or health) and should not be detrimental to (should preserve) the liberal values of clients and others in the society (Bayles, 1981:19).

The connections to democratic values stated herein are not compelling. They permit interpretation and balancing on the part of the professional beyond that which the police should have. The commitment to democratic values is stated as a third order obligation after obligations to personal and client interests. Also, the obligations are clearly cited as "should" rather than "must," which weakens their persuasive force. Therefore, political/social values may be ignored by the professional or placed in lower priority in respect to personal, client, or professional values.

Above, three differences have been identified between the professions and the police which argue for a different framework as the basis of police ethics and obligations. These include the public purpose of the police, the "must" nature of police obligations, and the clients that the police serve. First, the police are a public agency serving the public interest. They perform tasks that evolved out of the duties of citizenship which became too complex and time consuming for citizens to retain. Thus, their primary purpose is a public, not a private, one. A system of ethics for the police must account for this major difference.

The framework chosen must assist in the education of the police in "the attempt to make the agent responsive to the demands of the structure of authority within which he is to act" (Tussman, 1970:17). The authority granted to the police is not like that which is granted to a profession. The traditional professions can engage in their occupations in or out of government service. The police are creatures of government. They are solely public servants, in public agencies, operating from a grant of authority from the public for public purposes. This poses a structure of authority that requires the public purpose to be placed in the primary position when the police consider conflicts, or attempt balancing with personal, occupational, or other interests. For example, in situations of natural disaster, personal and occupational interests would permit the members of most professions to flee and remain uninvolved in the public response. Only those in public service or who choose to volunteer need remain in harm's way. While police might prefer to flee to safety, they do not have this choice. The police must place themselves at risk and may be given tasks not routinely assigned to the occupation. Thus, personal safety and normal occupational concerns are subordinated to the public interest.

Second, the obligations that the police assume are not posed in the nature of "should" or "ought to" but "has to" or "must." They are more binding than moral obligations. Le Baron (1967:69-71) describes abstract commitment as bringing about two types of obligations. One is to "those values, principles, rules to which we have become committed and which we regard as binding on all alike" or moral obligations. The other is legal obligation, which involves not just commitment to rules but commitment to the authority of a system generating the rules. However, both of these remain abstract. The obligations of the police are much more concrete.

> We believe that people ought to act within the boundaries set by moral concepts and see their choices in moral terms, but most of us also believe that public officials, because of the institutional stations they have assumed have committed themselves to an institutional duty to act in morally appropriate ways (French, 1983:10).

The "must" nature of police obligations extends from the institutional duty assumed within the social commitment of the oath of office. The oath is "a direct and explicit social act, such as agreement, consent or contract," which binds them (Le Baron, 1967:69). In the swearing of the oath, police obligations assume a "must" nature as the "three strands of obligation converge" (Le Baron, 1967:71). The oath establishes social commitment, has legally binding force like a contract, and carries the moral force of personal agreements. Heffernan (1985) has provided an excellent discussion of the binding nature of the police oath. The obligations accepted by the police official are not optional in nature as are those of the professional. Physicians may choose to perform abortions or not perform abortions based on their personal moral preferences, unfettered by professional values. In the same manner attorneys may refuse to represent abortion supporters. However, police officers assigned to help quell a disturbance at an abortion clinic, and so permit the clinic to operate cannot refuse to do so regardless of the strength of their personal opposition to abortion. Similarly, even with strong sympathy for the cause of striking union members, the police are obligated to protect the business the strike is against and any replacement workers it might hire.

Third, the police have a three-part clientele, which distinguishes their obligations from the traditional professions. Both the police and the professions obtain obligations when clients seek assistance within the scope of their occupational roles. In this one-on-one relationship, the obligations of the police can rightly be seen as similar to those of the traditional professional. However, police obligations to specific clients are secondary—they serve as a vehicle to perform tasks in relation to their primary obligation, the public interest.

While it is true that the professional ought to serve the public interest in serving the individual client, this is a secondary obligation. The physician's obligation is to the specific ill patient, not to all ill people. The lawyer's obligation is to the specific client in need of legal advice, not to all of those individuals seeking justice. However, the police have fundamental obligations to prevent crime, maintain public order, and to provide for the social welfare, whether or not specific clients have sought assistance. The traditional professional may not have an obligation to perform tasks unless activated by client demand, whereas police work may be characterized as oriented toward preventing specific client demand. The physician or lawyer assumes such obligations only when employed by a public agency.

A third client exists for the police which makes them significantly different from the traditional professions. Police officials are obligated to serve the interests of offenders by insuring due process guarantees and providing the substance of justice to these same individuals. This places offenders in a client relationship with the police. The obligation to offenders exists even though they may pose a threat to the general public or a specific client. Physicians have no similar obligation to the germ or virus that may infect the victim of disease. Attorneys do not have a similar obligation toward their clients' opponents.

When confronted with a patient held hostage by disease, the physician may seek to destroy the disease-causing agent without moral question. Collectively, physicians may seek to eradicate the organism from the planet as has been attempted with smallpox. In a hostage situation, the police may not take the life of the offender without first considering the general public interest in preservation of life that applies to both the hostage and the offender. Also, client-specific obligations to protect both lives exist. The police are placed in the difficult position of serving public, victim, and offender interests in a manner that maximizes each or otherwise does the least harm to each.

A framework for police ethics is needed that can account for these three separate clients, the public purpose of the police, and the "must" nature of police obligations.

The Political Obligation of the Police Agent

An appropriate framework for the development of police ethics is the theory of political obligation. I do not refer to the political obligation of the member of the body politic. The theory, as applied to members, seems to be fraught with controversy surrounding how the member assumes obligation. Instead, I refer to the political obligation of the agent who has consciously assumed the role of agent and intentionally accepted role obligations. For the police, this has been done by the swearing of the oath of office and in entering a contract with the police agency to provide work for pay and benefits.

"The political agent is one who is authorized to act on behalf of, or in the name of, others—the members, or the body politic" (Tussman, 1970:59). The police officer is such a political agent. The police officer is an employee of a public agency that obtains its authority, purpose, resources, and institutional structure from the body politic. The police act as agents by exercising discretionary decision-making and performing specific tasks that have been assigned to or adopted by the police institution. These duties are performed for, and in the name of, the citizens of the agency's governmental unit.

Within the obligations of the public agent, we find the connection between the role of the police and democratic values. The police officer, like the public "agent is responsible for a range of interests, goods, or purposes distinguishable from his own" which require the "subordination of private interest to public interest" (Tussman, 1970:59-60). These purposes are to be seen as the legitimate public purposes for which the institution and its subordinate roles were created and authorized by the body politic (Tussman, 1970:67-68). The police officer, as public agent, is not as much responsible for professional or private purposes as public ones, and thereby, the intended public values.

The police are further bound to democratic values and public purposes by the nature of the government within which they serve. The police are not an isolated agency performing tasks assigned solely to them. The police officer performs a role within an institution's role that is embedded in a system of institutions serving the same, similar, or related purposes. The structure of our government obligates the police to see their decisions and actions as related to other government systems and places an obligation of coordination upon them (Tussman, 1970:64). The police are one part of a complex set of social institutions established to protect and further social values.

Moreover, the systemic nature of our public institutions and the limited nature of authority given to them place an obligation upon public agents to conform their behavior to value-based principles such as the "separation of powers" and "checks and balances" (Tussman, 1970:66). Public agents must not operate outside the authority granted to them, but ought to demonstrate conformity to principles, law, and rules tied to their institution's purpose. Agents and agencies are bound by standards of appropriate procedure and propriety of method still evolving within our system. The public agent is required to "pursue the appropriate purpose with proper procedure and with respect to relevant law" (Tussman, 1970:67, 70-75).

This analysis leads to the conclusion that moral imperatives attach to the police occupation. These imperatives may dramatically affect analysis of hard choices and moral dilemmas in policing. Obligations such as balancing majority and minority interests, avoidance of tyranny, abiding by the rule of law, and enhancing the pursuits of life and liberty are not optional for public servants like the police. Therefore, they will find limiting boundaries to service toward any one public purpose derived from the necessity to serve other purposes. The police will find their hardest choices in the balancing of conflicting purposes and in integrating an unequivocal application of the limits on their power upon their actions. Several examples may be useful at this point.

In a situation in which knowledge about a drug dealer's intent to kill a rival dealer comes reliably to the police, several options are available. The police might warn both dealers to prevent the crime, attempt to trap the first in the act, or let the murder of the second occur and arrest the first on capital charges. The last option would remove two criminals from the society and contribute to the public interest in order. However, only the first option can be completely ethical. The obligations to protect individuals, avoid tyranny, and extend the values of life and liberty equally limit police in service of public order. The obligation to protect life and liberty extends even to members of devalued minority groups such as drug dealers and places an unavoidable limit on police behavior. The prevention of the potential crime preserves order and both the life of one citizen and the liberty of the other.

Where police action in service of public purpose is barred by purpose-imposed law and procedure, action in their disregard is immoral action. Here it is useful to extend the drug dealing example to the often-discussed issue of dirty means in service of moral goods (see Heffernan, 1982:32; Klockars, 1983; Pollock-Byrne, 1989:94-95). The police may believe that incarceration of dealers is a significant moral good, peace, or order. Investigative difficulties may lead to the adoption of dirty means, the planting of evidence, lying to obtain warrants, or torture to obtain evidence, in service of that good. However, peace and order are limited values in this society. They are limited by the fundamental nature of our government and by the diversity of interests present that must receive balanced response from government. In acting through dirty means in a specific instance, the police commit an immoral act. If these choices of dirty means for specific cases become a frequent, systematic, occupationally accepted practice, the police become agents of tyranny, not democracy. The acceptance of their political obligations to provide liberty and justice for all clients, to avoid tyranny, and to conform their behavior to the rule of law, denies to the police any dirty means.

The imperative nature of police obligations also extends to the issue of loyalty to peers (see Wren, 1985). What must officers do who know of peer misbehavior?

They should demonstrate loyalty to their peers and to occupational solidarity. However, these are optional obligations and must be subordinated to police obligations to clients and public purposes. When integrated into the obligations of a public agent, loyalty to peers becomes the duty to assist each other in conformity to the demands of their office, to prevent and correct misbehavior, and to report if these fail. This form of loyalty preserves public purposes, the careers of peers, and valid occupational relationships to clients.

Perhaps the imperatives of service to democracy lead to a modification of the role relationship between the police and society. The nature of crime fighting or crime control strategies in the service of social peace and order may contribute to the denial of limits and the rejection of the need to balance interests. The police need to develop a role that permits them to balance a multitude of interests, reject dirty means, and not just preserve, but enhance and extend democratic values. Crime prevention through techniques of problem-solving as described by Goldstein (1990) may permit the development of a role relationship consistent with police obligations.

At this point, we can note that the concept of political accounts for the public nature of the police purpose because it casts the police official as a public agent it permits us to view the social and political obligations of the police in terms of "must" because police accept their agency through oath and contract. Also, it accounts for their responsibilities to the public, to specific clients who request service, and to the offender whose rights must be preserved. Finally, political obligation ties the police to democratic values.

The Need for Representative Bureaucracy in Policing

To act as required, the public agent must be conversant with values widely held by the body politic. We would want agents to have frequent and purposeful communication with the members of the body politic to refresh their understanding of evolving democratic values. This requirement mitigates against the development of professional autonomy and would encourage efforts to eliminate police isolation from the public. Autonomy of government agencies is in direct opposition to the nature of democracy. The police need to seek a relationship with the society that does not separate and isolate, but involves and binds both.

Two aspects of the agent's position led to this conclusion. First, "the agent claims certain basic 'powers' necessary for the adequate discharge of his duty" and foremost among them may be the power of discretion (Tussman, 1970:61-62). If we were to perform the duties or make the decisions which the agent performs for us, we would most likely survive to do these as well as we could. Logically, we would expect agents to act on our behalf to the best of their ability. "The representative, the public agent, had better be us at our best, not at our most typical" (Tussman, 1970:62). Beyond this, since the police agent is trained in the occupation, we would expect better performance of their role than we could provide. Part of this better performance should be a better understanding and application to action of appropriate purpose. This better understanding can only come if the agent is well educated about the public interest(s) and values that create the foundation for that purpose, law, and procedure. These values could be found within information exchanged between the public and the police should adequate channels for exchange be created.

Second, "the actions of the agent, in the name of the body politic, are binding upon the members and create obligations for them" (Tussman, 1970:59). Police officers create policy and operationalize the law to some extent by their decisions and actions. They expend the resources granted to them by the public, while creating specific obligations for citizens through their powers to direct citizen behavior or require actions in order to receive services. These uses of authority and resources and the potential obligation of citizens to act require the police to inform and involve the public in decisionmaking and action.

This analysis leads to the conclusion that the police ought to form representative bureaucracies instead of pursuing an isolated autonomous profession. Mosher (1968:1) and Lorch (1980:217) have observed that most decisions and actions performed by government and much of the legislative and judicial powers exercised are in the hands of appointed administrative employees. This places a significant barrier to democratic processes. One may argue that representativeness can be obtained by the attempt to hire representative people and to insure that the education of administrators deals adequately with the values of the society (see Mosher, 1968). However, neither of these mechanisms can adequately produce representativeness because both are inherently selective. The integration of democratic processes within public administration is a necessity.

Although Finer (1941) and Friedrich (1942) disagree as to the nature of the administrator's responsibility to the public, they both argue that some form of political direction and communication from the public is necessary for public administration in a democracy. Lorch (1980:100) uses the phrase "democratic administration" and notes that "[i]t is a method of carrying on the administrative process in such a way as to encourage participation . . . . in the decision-making process by those affected by the decision. Consultation is the heart of democratic administration." The police as a public bureaucracy have a representative responsibility and must be in communication with the public. They must find institutional methods for allowing and encouraging information flow from the public. Such methods will of necessity reduce the occupation's isolation and chances of autonomy. The form of the police institution under these concepts would be dramatically different from that which now exists.

Policy Making, Citizen Participation and Participatory Management

Applying the concepts of public agency delineated above permits justification for several developments in police administration: openness in policy making, citizen participation in police tasks, and participatory management.

"Constitutional democracy is based on the political responsibility of the individual citizen, because it rests on the consent of most of the governed . . . . Constitutional democracy is based also on the responsibility of governments to their electorates" (Spiro, 1969:28-29). This responsibility underlies the development of openness in policy making, greater citizen participation in accomplishment of agency goals, and increased employee participation in management.

Two aspects of this responsibility bear directly upon the need for openness in police administration and policy making. First, the government has a duty "to determine policies, to carry on programs in realization of policies, and to explain to, and educate the citizens about, those policies, programs, and the problems that lie in and behind them" (Appleby, 1962). This duty is found in the right to self-government and in the notice required within the rule of law as a right to information (Bedau, 1981). Indeed,

> [s]elf-government is impossible without a responsible citizenship. Any people which is uninformed, ignorant, shortsighted, inattentive to ideas or events, which has no capacity for independent decision, which has no defense against emotional contagion, which is fickle and gullible, is not prepared for the hard task of self-government (Dykstra, 1939:24).

Also, Margolis (1981:243) argues that this adequate information would permit citizens to

> function both as a source for recruiting informed members of the government and as competent to exercise their rights and powers within the private sector; they can function effectively in neither of these capacities without suitable access to pertinent information.

Second, democracy is served not only by informing the public, but by providing access to communicate to administrators and to participate directly in governing. True "democracy in rule-making is served by opening the doors of public participation as widely as possible" (Lorch, 1980:103). Sharp (1980:105-106) argues for the adoption of the co-production model where possible because "[i]t expands the public official's role from one of performing and being called to account to one that also includes recognizing and developing citizen competencies." It involves developing competence toward self-government and in accomplishing tasks directed at fulfilling the agency's purpose.

Langton (1979:410) notes the growth of bureaucracy and the complexity of society as facts which require ways

> to make that bureaucracy more responsive to the needs and sentiments of the people it serves. It is for this reason that citizen involvement has become a necessary facet of governmental administration. Citizen involvement is no more or less than the need of the administrative state to conform to the representative democratic tradition in America.

The police cannot perform their duties without the cooperation and assistance of the public. Sharp (1980:1-10) argues for the further "recognition that public services are the joint product of the activities of both citizens and government officials." An example of this co-production is the joint work required in crime prevention tough block watches (Sharp, 1980:116).

Finally, the concept of political obligation leads us to participatory forms of management for police agencies. Mosher (1968:17-18) summarizes a number of organizational and individual benefits obtained through greater employee participation: better decisions, better morale, greater self-actualization of employees, greater effectiveness and efficiency, a higher degree of commitment, and development of democratic ideals. Even though these benefits may be compelling, the agent's individual or personal responsibility provides sufficient reason for participatory management. Denhardt (1977) points out "to the extent that we are to be held accountable for a particular action, we should participate fully in the formulation of that role." The democratic responsibilities of the police should encourage the individual officer to seek participation within the police organization and, barred from that, to seek to influence the organization through unions and associations. Ultimately, the police should actively engage in politics as suggested by Muir (1983).

Participatory management permits the police to internally practice democratic values required externally by their role. Pateman (1975:18-19) indicates that "[t]he aim of organizational democracy is democracy . . . . it is to further justice, equality, freedom, the rights of citizens, and the protection of the interests of citizens." Indeed, in a complex, technical bureaucratic environment, it is the "participatory approach to organizational democracy that is likely to foster the expertise, skills, and confidence . . . . that are vital" (Pateman, 1975:21).

To this point, I have purposely not cited current examples of democratic administration within American policing. However, goals of professionalization, improving productivity and service delivery, and improving the public image of police found within the occupation, encourage the development of administrative methods supportive of the three democratic ends discussed above. Skolnick and Bayley (1986) cite several examples of openness to public participation in policy-making, cooperative efforts to provide police services, and decentralized, participatory management. The development of community-oriented and problem-solving policing techniques are to be encouraged for their potential to improve police services. However, their importance may be in their potential to improve the quality of democracy within American society (Kelling, 1988, Kelling & Stewart, 1989).

Summary

In a democratic society, police ethics must find their foundation within the values that provide society's foundation. We must seek a framework for the study of police ethics that encourages our consideration of democratic values and democratic processes. This is so because the purpose for the police and the grant of authority that creates them come from the body politic.

I have argued that traditional discussions of professional ethics fail to provide a model adequate to support the connection between democratic values and police ethics. Traditional professional ethics do not account for the public nature of the police occupation. They fail to develop the primacy of the public interest, do not cast the obligations on police in a strong enough mode, and do not account for the complex nature of the police clientele.

A workable framework for the development of police ethics is found in the theory of political obligation. The police should be characterized as public agent's with political obligations. This model recognizes the public purpose of the police as the primary function against which all other interests must be measured and balanced. The theory of political obligation characterizes the police as agents of the public, recognizes the existence of specific clients, and requires acceptance of the offender as a client. The theory of political obligation also permits the obligations of the police role to be viewed as "must" conditions rather than weaker "should" considerations. The police official/public agent has assumed social, legal, and moral obligations upon entering this occupation. The political obligations of the police bind them to fundamental democratic values.

The police role, when recognized as that of a public agent, places an obligation on police agencies and police officials to behave so as to bring basic democratic values to life. The police role requires the development of representative/democratic forms of organization to encourage citizen participation in democratic processes. For these reasons, the theory of political obligation is recommended as a viable framework to link police activities to the demands of a democratic society. This framework poses the possibility that the forces of order may evolve into agents of democracy rather than agents of tyranny.

Note

Research for this article was partially funded by an Organized Faculty Research Grant from Corpus Christi State University. This is a revision the paper originally presented at The Academy of Criminal Justice Sciences meeting, April 7, 1988 in San Francisco, California.

References

Appleby, P. (1962). *Citizens As Sovereigns.* Syracuse, NY: Syracuse University Press.

Bayles, M. (1981). *Professional Ethics.* Belmont, CA: Wadsworth.

Bedau, H. (1981). The Government's Responsibility to Inform the Public. In N. Bowie (ed.), *Ethical Issues in Government.* Philadelphia, PA: Temple University Press.

Broderick, J. (1987). *Police in a Time of Change,* (2nd ed.). Prospect Heights, IL: Waveland Press.

Camenish, P. (1983). *Grounding Professional Ethics in a Pluralistic Society.* New York, NY: Haven.

Delaney, H. (1990). Toward a Police Professional Ethic." In F. Schmalleger (ed.), *Ethics In Criminal Justice.* Bristol, IN: Wyndham Hall.

Delattre, E. (1989). *Character and Cops: Ethics in Policing.* Washington, DC: American Enterprise Institute for Public Policy Research.

Denhardt, R. (1977). "Individual Responsibility in an Age of Organization." *Midwest Review of Public Administration,* 11,4:259-269.

Dykstra, C. (1939). "The Quest for Responsibility." *American Political Science Review,* 33(February): 1-25.

Elliston, F. and N. Bowie (1982). *Ethics, Public Policy and Criminal Justice.* Cambridge, MA: Oelgeschlager, Gunn and Hain.

Finer, H. (1941). "Administrative Responsibility in Democratic Government." *Public Administration Review,* 1,4:335-350.

French, P. (1983). *Ethics in Government.* Englewood Cliffs, NJ: Prentice-Hall.

Friedrich, C. (1942). *The New Belief in the Common Man.* Boston, MA: Little, Brown.

_________ (1968). *Constitutional Government and Democracy: Theory and Practice in Europe and America,* (4th ed.). Waltham, MA: Blaisdell.

Gawthrop, L. (1984). *Public Sector Management, Systems, and Ethics.* Bloomington, IN: Indiana University Press.

Goldstein, H. (1977). *Policing a Free Society.* Cambridge, MA: Ballinger.

________ (1990). *Problem-Oriented Policing.* New York, NY: McGraw-Hill.

Gustafson, R. (1981). "Toward an Ethic for the System in Criminal Justice." In F. Schmalleger and R. Gustafson (eds.), *The Social Basis of Criminal Justice: Ethical Issues for the 80's.* Washington, DC: University Press of America.

Heffernan, W. (1982). "Two Approaches to Police Ethics." *Criminal Justice Review,* 7,1:28-35.

________ (1985). "The Police and Their Rules of Office: An Ethical Analysis." In W. Heffernan and T. Stroup (eds.), *Police Ethics: Hard Choices in Law Enforcement.* New York, NY: John Jay Press.

Johnson, C. and G. Copus (1981). "Law Enforcement Ethics: A Theoretical Analysis." In F. Schmalleger and R. Gustafson (eds.), *The Social Basis of Criminal Justice: Ethical Issues for the 80's.* Washington, DC: University Press of America.

Kelling, G. (1988). *Police and Communities: The Quiet Revolution.* Washington, DC: National Institute of Justice.

________ and J. Stewart (1989). *Neighborhoods and the Police: The Maintenance of Civil Authority.* Washington, DC: National Institute of Justice.

Klockars, C. (1983). "The Dirty Harry Problem." In C. Klockars (ed.), *Thinking About Police: Contemporary Readings.* New York, NY: McGraw-Hill.

Langton, S. (1979). "American Citizen Participation: A Deep-Rooted Tradition." *National Civic Review,* 68,8:403-411, 422.

Le Baron, B. (1967). "Real and Mythic Obligations." *Ethics,* 78,1:62-76.

________ (1973). "Three Components of Political Obligation." *Canadian Journal of Political Science,* 6,3:478-493.

Lilla, M. (1981) "Ethos, 'Ethics,' and Public Service." *The Public Interest,* 63(Spring):3-17.

Lorch, R. (1980). *Democratic Process and Administrative Law,* (rev. ed.). Detroit, MI: Wayne State University Press.

Margolis, J. (1981). "Democracy and the Responsibility to Inform the Public." In N. Bowie (ed.), *Ethical Issues in Government.* Philadelphia, PA: Temple University Press.

Metz, H. (1990). "An Ethical Model for Law Enforcement Administrators." In F. Schmalleger (ed.), *Ethics in Criminal Justice.* Bristol, IN: Wyndham Hall.

More, H. (1985). "Police Professionalism: Introduction." In H. More, Jr. (ed.) *Critical Issues in Law Enforcement,* 4th ed. Cincinnati, OH: Anderson Publishing Co.

Mosher, F (1968). *Democracy and the Public Service.* New York, NY: Oxford University Press.

Muir, W., Jr. (1983). "Police and Politics." *Criminal Justice Ethics*, 2,2:3-9.

Myrdal, G. (1962). *An American Dilemma*. New York, NY: Harper and Row.

Newman, D. and P. Anderson (1989). *Introduction to Criminal Justice*, 4th ed. New York, NY: Random House.

Pateman, C. (1975). "A Contribution to the Political Theory of Organizational Democracy." *Administration and Society* 7,1:5-26.

Pollock-Byrne, J. (1989). *Ethics in Crime and Justice: Dilemmas & Decisions*. Pacific Grove, CA: Brooks/Cole.

Price, B. (1977). *Police Professionalism Rhetoric and Action*. Lexington, MA: Lexington Books.

Schmalleger, F. and R. Gustafson, eds. (1981). *The Social Basis of Criminal Justice: Ethical Issues for the 80s*. Washington, DC: University Press of America.

Sharp, E. (1980). "Toward a New Understanding of Urban Services and Citizen Participation: The Co-production Concept." *Midwest Review of Public Administration*, 14,2:105-118.

Sherman, L. (1981). *The Study of Ethics in Criminology and Criminal Justice Curricula*. Washington, DC: Joint Commission on Criminology and Criminal Justice Education and Standards.

_________ (1982). *Ethics in Criminal Justice Education*. New York, NY: Hastings on Hudson.

Skolnick, J. and D. Bayley (1986). *The New Blue Line: Police Innovation in Six American Cities*. New York, NY: The Free Press.

Spiro, H. (1969). *Responsibility in Government*. New York, NY: Van Nostrand Reinhold.

Tussman, J. (1970). *Obligation and the Body Politic*. New York, NY: Oxford University Press.

Walker, S. (1983). *The Police in America: An Introduction*. New York, NY: McGraw-Hill.

Wren, T. (1974). *Agency and Urgency: The Origin of Moral Obligation*. New York, NY: Precedent Publishers.

_________ (1985). "Whistle-Blowing and Loyalty to One's Friends." In W. Heffernan and T. Stroup (eds.) *Police Ethics: Hard Choices in Law Enforcement*. New York, NY: John Jay Press.

Police Administration in the Future: Demographic Influences as they Relate to Management of the Internal and External Environment

Jack E. Enter
Gwinnett County Sheriff's Department

Few would deny that American law enforcement today must deal with a myriad of management-related problems. Issues concerning jail overcrowding, financial limitations, lawsuits, and other forms of organizational dilemmas have placed more stress upon the police manager of today than perhaps in any other era of history.

Though change has always been a part of American history, the change of today seems much more dynamic and frequent. Whereas change in the past was often discussed in terms of decades, if not centuries, the change today seems to occur from year to year. Naisbitt, in his book *Megatrends* (1982:95), summed up this new era of change by likening it to a world where "the very ground is shifting beneath us." *Megatrends* and its sequel, *Reinventing the Corporation* (1985), became best sellers as the private sector sought to deal with this change.

Given the pace of change of today and certainly in the future, the problems of the criminal justice system will be at least as complex as those facing the private sector. With this in mind, the purpose of this article is twofold. The first objective is to examine present trends and future projections in order to better prepare the manager and the student of the American police to predict the changes that will impact this system. Second, by examining the future, we will hopefully provide insight into the current policies and practices of law enforcement agencies and how they will (or will not) fare in the light of the year 2000.

Section I: The Dimensions of Change

What Factors Influence Change?

When examining the past and the present, we note several factors or variables that have facilitated change. The *economic* well-being of a state, region, or the country at large has a significant impact upon crime and social conditions, as well as upon the ability of the criminal justice system to respond to these needs. Another factor of change has been in the area of legal institutions and the *law.* The impact of the Warren Court upon American law enforcement was a substantial change agent upon American policing, as would be the more conservative approaches of the Burger and the Rehnquist courts. *Technology* has been influential as well. The American police were forever changed by the advent of the patrol car, the two-way radio, and other technological advances that will continue to change future operations of law enforcement.

Ultimately, however, one of the more potent variables of change has to do with *people.* Given the many responsibilities of law enforcement, the type of people with which it must deal externally (citizens, especially victims and perpetrators) and internally (sworn and non-sworn personnel) is very likely the most important dimension of change.

The focus of this article is to examine these "people changes" as they pertain to the variables of *age, race, and gender.* Once these demographic trends are discussed, we will speculate upon how these changes affect crime and influence police management today, and we will also speculate upon anticipated changes in the future.

Demographic Trend #1: The Aging of America

Crime has usually been associated with youth. The young males of the United States have traditionally been responsible for the majority of crime. In 1986, 58.3 percent of all arrests were of individuals in the age range of 16-29. This statistic has been more or less consistent over time (Flanagan & Jamieson, 1988:317). The number of individuals in that particular age category is therefore important when one looks at crime and criminal justice. This was dramatically illustrated when the "baby-boomers" entered this age bracket in American society in the 1960s and the 1970s. As crime rates skyrocketed, crime and criminal justice became the focus of the public, the media, and governmental commissions.

America has traditionally been a youth-oriented nation. This tradition, however, is beginning to change. The maturation of the "baby-boomers," smaller nuclear families, and an extended life expectancy are contributing to that change. The average American is living longer, the general population is becoming older, and the percentage of young people is decreasing. The following table illustrates the growth and decline of various age categories of the American population.

Table 1
U.S. Population Change, 1980-1987

Age	Percent Change
Under 5 years	+ 11.6
5 to 13 years	− 1.1
14 to 17 years	− 11.0
18 to 24 years	− 9.7
25 to 34 years	+ 16.8
35 to 44 years	+ 33.8
45 to 54 years	+ 2.1
55 to 64 years	+ 1.5
65 to 74 years	+ 13.4
75 to 84 years	+ 20.3
85+ years	+ 28.0
All ages	+ 7.4

Source: Miller, 1988: x.

The trends in Table 1 are further substantiated by the fact that in 1977, 3.15 million Americans graduated from high school, while in 1993 only 2.5 million are expected to do the same. These figures represent a marked decline of 27 percent (Naisbitt & Aburdene, 1985:174). Projections by the U.S. Census Bureau estimate that "more than a quarter of the population will be aged sixty years and older by the year 2025" (Bennett, 1987:57). This aging of the American population, combined with a dwindling pool of the young, will probably influence the criminal justice system in several ways. These consequences will be discussed in Sections II and III.

Demographic Trend #2: From "Either-Or" to "Multiple Option"

In *Megatrends,* John Naisbitt identified the changing of our society from "either-or" scenarios to those involving multiple options as one of his megatrends.

This multidimensional environment of the future will be especially evident in the arena of race or ethnic composition of American society. When discussing crime or personnel issues in the past, the demographics of the people involved have normally been confined to white and black males. Crimes and crime data have often been limited to these "either-or" categories, as well as in personnel issues such as hiring and promotions. But the criminal justice system of 1990 and beyond is no longer quite that "either-or."

American criminology and law enforcement have been substantially influenced by immigration throughout their history. The large influx of predominantly European immigrants during the last century and the early twentieth century was much of the impetus behind the creation of the American police, as well as the focus of early criminological theorists and sociologists. Immigrants (and migrating native-born Americans) influenced not only the type of criminal and the type of victim dealt with by the American police, but these individuals would become the labor pool and personnel of these same agencies in the future. The era of the great influx of the European immigrants is past, but now we must examine the immigrants of today and tomorrow.

Though individuals will continue to enter the United States from Eastern and Western Europe, the bulk of new immigrants (80 percent) will come from Asia and Latin America (Tomasi, 1989:9). As seen in Table 2, European and Canadian immigrants represented only 13.5 percent of legal aliens who entered the United States from 1981 to 1985; in 1951-1960, Europe and Canada had provided the majority of immigrants. Immigration from Asia has also increased markedly, rising from only 6.1 percent in 1951-1960 to almost one-half of all immigrants in 1981-1985. Asian-Americans, whose 1980 population in the United States was 3.4 million, are expected to triple in representation during this decade. Even now, Asian-Americans outnumber blacks in California (Tomasi, 1989:9). The ethnic composition of the Asian-American population for 1980 and projections for the future are contained in Table 3.

Table 2
Legal Alien Immigration by Country or Region: Percentage of Immigrants by Time Period

Time Period	Europe and Canada	Asia	Mexico	Latin America	Other
1951-1960	66.1%	6.1%	11.9%	14.3%	1.6%
1961-1970	46.3%	12.9%	13.7%	25.6%	1.5%
1971-1980	21.6%	35.3%	14.2%	26.1%	2.8%
1981-1985	13.5%	47.8%	11.7%	23.7%	3.3%

Source: Passell, 1986, Figure 5.

Table 3
Asian-American Population: 1980 and Projections for 1990 and 2000 (in millions)*

	1980	1990	2000
All Asian-Americans	3.47	6.53	9.95
Chinese	.81	1.26	1.68
Filipino	.78	1.41	2.07
Japanese	.72	.80	.85
Asian Indian	.39	.68	1.01
Korean	.36	.81	1.32
Vietnamese	.25	.68	1.57
Other Asian	.17	.71	1.34

Source: Tomasi, 1989:10.

The other major category of immigration consists of Hispanics. The Hispanic population in the United States has increased by 34 percent (or 5 million) since the 1980 census. In 1988, Hispanics constituted 8.1 percent of the population, as compared to 6.5 percent in 1980 (Del Pinal, 1988:1). If present trends continue, that segment of the population will reach 47 million by 2020 (Tomasi, 1989:10). As Table 2, most of that increase will continue to come from Latin American countries other than Mexico. In 1988, more than one-half (55 percent) of Hispanics lived in California and Texas (Del Pinal, 1988:2). From 1987 to 2000, it is estimated that California, Texas, and Florida will account for more than one-half of the total U.S. population increase (Wetrogen, 1988:1). Much of the growth in these three states will undoubtedly contribute to Hispanic population trends.

As the population growth among blacks steadily increases into the twenty-first century, this segment of our population is projected to expand by 50 percent by the year 2030 (Spencer, 1989:1). According to Census Bureau estimates, blacks will increase as a percent of the total population from 12.4 in 1990 to 16.3 in 2080, while in the same period, the white population will decrease from 84.1 to 72.6 percent.

These demographic trends among the various racial and ethnic groups will result in the increasing diversification of American society. By 2010, "more than one-third of all American children will be black, Hispanic, or Asian" (Trojanowicz & Carter, 1990:61). Texas, now nearly 23 percent Hispanic, is expected to contain no ethnic majority by 2015 (Tomasi, 1989:9). The United States and American law enforcement will see the continued transformation from a society in which issues and crime-related problems were primarily two-dimensional (white and black) in context to one that is multidimensional (white, black, Hispanic, and Asian).

Demographic Trend #3: Expansion of the Role of Women

A demographic variable that remains relatively consistent over time concerns the percentage of females in the American population. Presently, females make up approximately 50 percent of the population, and it is reasonable to assume that this estimate will remain relatively constant in the future. The role of women in crime and as police personnel has never matched their demographic profile. With regard to their involvement in crime, females represented only 17.4 percent of all persons arrested in 1986 (Flanagan & Jamieson, 1988:374). Though women entering employment in law enforcement agencies has risen significantly in the past two decades, only 21.1 percent of all police employees (including civilian employees) in 1986 were females (Flanagan & Jamieson, 1988:30). These statistics are especially significant, considering the fact that in today's private sector employment representation among women and men in their 20s and 30s is almost identical (Naisbitt & Aburdene, 1985:208).

Section II: Crime Trends, The External Environment

The demographic trends described in Section I will obviously change the nature of the victims, perpetrators, and the public with which the criminal justice system of the future must relate. In Section II, we will examine four crime trends that are based upon the variables of age, race, and gender changes in American society.

Crime Trend #1: The Elderly Perpetrator

As mentioned earlier, crime has predominantly been associated with the young. As the population of America becomes increasingly older, the number of older citizens who are involved in crime will probably increase as well. Arrests of individuals aged 55 and older doubled between 1970 and 1980 (Bennett, 1987:57). Between the years 1976 and 1986, index property crimes among individuals aged 60 and older increased by 45 percent, while violent index crime among this group remained the same (Parisi, Gottfredson, Hindelang & Flanagan, 1977:482; Flanagan & Jamieson, 1988:372).

Georgette Bennett, in her book *Crimewarps*, discusses a potential increase in violent crimes and sex-related crimes (often involving the fondling of children) by the elderly segment of our population (pp. 62-63). Bennett believes that much of this increase will be attributed to behavior resulting from brain impairment and disorders that accompany old age. As the life expectancy of Americans increases, thus leading to a higher percentage of elderly persons in the population, the incidence of the "geriatric delinquent" will undoubtedly become a greater problem for the criminal justice system.

If Bennett's predictions are correct, one of the dilemmas that the criminal justice system will face concerns the processing of the older criminal through our present system. Arrest and detention policies, culpability issues, and sentencing options of today are limited in their ability to deal with the unique problems posed by elderly criminals. This gap will be especially apparent in issues concerning long-term incarceration of the elderly who will require extensive medical and psychological care beyond the present capabilities of most correctional institutions. As law enforcement agencies face increased contacts with elderly offenders, it is likely that the other components of our criminal justice system will be ill-prepared for the referrals by police of the geriatric criminal.

Crime Trend #2: The Elderly Victim

Though it is generally known that the elderly fear crime more than any other segment of our population (Lindquist & Duke, 1987:55), they have generally been the group least likely to be victimized. Persons aged 65 and older have the lowest rate of victimization in this country, both with regard to violent and property crimes (McCaghy & Cernkovich, 1987:67). As mentioned earlier, by the year 2025, more than one-quarter of the population will be 60 or older. Therefore, it would be logical to assume that victimization of this age group will substantially increase, simply because the elderly will represent the greatest target population for the criminally minded. This is especially true because the elderly have become one of the more wealthy segments of our population. Although they presently constitute only one-sixth of the population, America's elderly "own one-third of all household net worth and 40 percent of financial assets" (Naisbitt & Aburdene, 1990:45).

Though many of the increases in victimization would involve property crimes, especially in regard to fraud and "con games," it is likely that the elderly will also experience greater victimization by violent crime. Some "targeting" of the elderly victim has already been seen among serial murderers and serial rapists (gerontophilia). Another probable increase in violent crime against the elderly will be in the area of "granny bashing," that is, domestic violence against the elderly. This is especially likely to occur if the continued growth of the aged population places greater economic burdens on the younger and less numerous American working couples.

What impact will the elderly victim have upon the American police? First, given the pronounced fear of crime by the elderly, the calls for service-related tasks (i.e., checking for prowlers) will probably increase for law enforcement agencies. Second, on a more positive note, the increased use of the elderly in "crime watch" programs and other voluntary roles in criminal justice is likely to rise. The use of senior citizens to provide volunteer services in police departments and sheriffs offices has a significant potential not only to obtain assistance in routine tasks but also to co-opt the elderly community (often one of the more politically active groups) as a means of garnering public support for these agencies.

Crime Trend #3: Less Youth = Less Crime?

It would seem logical that as the percentage of youth among the American population decreases, that there should be a corresponding decrease in crime. Unfortunately, if this trend is to be realized at all, it will be to a very limited degree. Why? First, although there are already fewer young people today than a decade ago, our crime rate has not decreased to a significant degree; conversely, after a brief decline during the period 1981-1985, it is on the increase. Second, as mentioned in *Crime Trend #1*, the elderly will likely increase in their representation among persons arrested for crime. The most significant reason for a continued increase in crime will likely originate in social and economic trends of today and the future. These variables, as they are affected by demographic trends, will now be examined.

Some criminologists and other students of the social environment believe that the United States is heading toward an increased polarization between the "haves" and the "have-nots" (McCord & Wicker, 1990; Tafoya, 1987; Cole, 1989). One of the more significant reasons for this projected polarization has to do with America's continued transformation from a nation based upon industry to one based upon "information"—that related to computer and other information-based businesses (Naisbitt, 1982). As well-paying employment opportunities increase, becoming more sophisticated and technologically based, individuals (especially minorities) with limited educational and training backgrounds will find themselves isolated in menial or labor-intensive jobs (Toffler & Toffler, 1990). Even obtaining the lower-paying jobs will potentially be more difficult, especially for black and Hispanic males. The reasons for this include the continued increase of women in the work force, as well as the influx of immigrants into this country, as this combination will make competition for these jobs severe. It has been projected that only 15 percent of those entering the labor force in this country during the next 13 years will he native-born males (Tomasi, 1989:8).

What will be the result of this economic disparity upon crime in America? Most likely the result will be more crime, and that crime will often be racially or ethnically based. Youth and adult organized criminal gangs will likely continue to become a major form of criminal activity in the future, especially those involving violent crimes. This is especially true, given that many of the young Americans in the near future will be black, Hispanic, and Asian. Organized crime groups, such as Asian "triads" (criminal syndicates), will become the new "Cosa Nostra" of the 1990s and beyond (Bennett, 1987:81).

Potentially, some of these new forms of violent crime will be interracial. As the various ethnic and racial groups described in Part 1 become more numerous and competitive, the possibility of inter-minority violence may increase. There have already been incidents of riots and other forms of violence directed against other minority groups, and this is likely to continue into the future (Bennett, 1987).

Another factor that will influence violent crime in the future will be more generalization throughout American society. Though there are fewer young people today than in the past, studies seem to indicate some of these teen offenders "will be more chronically violent" (Bennett, 1987:52). In Bennett's book *Crimewarps*, it is reported that comparison of two birth cohorts found that the rate of violent crime among delinquents increased threefold in a generation" (p. 52). When we combine increased propensity towards violence with an increased economic polarization for much of America, the possibility of a decrease in crime seems unlikely.

Crime Trend #4: The Female Criminal

As crime generally has been recognized as a product of the young, it has also been a traditionally male phenomenon. Although females make up more than 50 percent of the population, they make up only a small percentage of those arrested for crimes. For instance, females are only arrested for one out of every ten violent crimes, and that number has been fairly consistent over time (Bennett, 1987:27). As women increase in the workplace, however, their opportunity to commit property crimes is likely to increase. As seen in Table 4, females as a percentage of all individuals arrested for crime, especially business-related property crime, is on the increase. There has also been an increase in arrests of women for violent crimes" of 22 percent between 1971 and 1985 (Bennett, 1987:30).

Table 4
Female Arrestees as Percentage of all Persons Arrested, by Crime

Offense	1971	1986
All Offenses	15.0%	17.4%
Fraud	28.6%	43.2%
Embezzlement	25.5%	36.8%

Source: Hindelang, Dunn, Sutton & Aumick, 1973, Flanagan & Jamieson, 1988.

Section III: Management Trends, The Internal Environment

The demographic trends discussed in Section I will also impact the internal environment of the criminal justice system. The next section will examine how the demographic trends of age, race, and gender will affect personnel matters within our law enforcement agencies.

Management Trend #1: A New Employee Profile

Until the recent past, the majority of police officers, probation officers, and other employees of the criminal justice system were white males. Issues in the last two decades concerning minority recruitment and promotion have attempted to change this dominance of the white male to a situation in which blacks, females, and other minorities have a greater representation among the criminal justice work force. This trend is likely to continue and will become more diversified in the future for several reasons.

First, the decreased number of young people from which to recruit new criminal justice employees will make competition in this area more intense with other public sector organizations and the private sector. For women who seek law enforcement careers and promotional opportunities, this trend will likely be most advantageous. Police agencies, whether or not they philosophically embrace this issue, will not be able to neglect one-half of the American population in the future competitive labor market.

Minorities will probably profit for the same reasons, especially in the area of Asian and Hispanic recruitment. The increase of minority representation in law enforcement agencies, therefore, is mainly attributed to simple mathematics: a smaller labor pool of young white males will numerically make the hiring and promotional practices of the past nearly impossible. In the private sector, less than one-half of all American workers are white males (Naisbitt & Aburdene, 1990:93). The police employee of the future will probably be representative of this trend as well.

Another factor that will influence the increased representation of minorities will result from those minorities currently working in law enforcement agencies. As these minorities attain more leadership positions within various criminal justice agencies, the philosophical resistance to minority issues should lessen to some degree. For example, female police chiefs will likely substantiate and increase female representation and recognition within the American police community.

Another concern for the future is whether or not collective bargaining and employee rights issues will be *between* the various minority groups. Will future employee litigation involving promotional opportunities and other employee issues be between Hispanics and blacks, or Asians and females—much like the criminal gang conflict along racial lines? Given that sonic employee groups among police departments are already formed along these lines, such inter-minority competition in these agencies is a possibility.

Management Trend #2: The Issue of the Veteran Employee

Another trend that is likely to occur as the result of the aging of America concerns the role and the rights of the older employee in the law enforcement agency. In the past, many agencies have not geared their recruitment and fiscal policies to benefit the middle-aged employee. A great number of law enforcement agencies have excluded the middle-aged person from seeking a position through "maximum age" restrictions, such as the exclusion of individuals 36 and older from being hired as federal agents in the Federal Bureau of Investigation. In the same manner, many agencies (especially at the federal level) have a mandatory retirement age (usually 55) for law enforcement employees.

Another age-related issue in police agencies has been the practice of limiting merit increases to the first seven or eight years of an individual's career. After that time has passed, the employee "tops out" in his or her ability to obtain annual salary increases other than through promotions or through increases given to all personnel, agency-wide.

These age-related personnel policies of the past are likely to be modified for several reasons. First, the aging of America will probably make such policies a political liability. Given the numerical and therefore political representation of the middle-aged and elderly citizens among the American public, we are likely to see increased legal scrutiny of personnel practices that might be seen as discriminatory toward this age group.

Another reason for the future modifications of policies unfavorable to the veteran employee will be the aforementioned problems in the areas of recruitment and training, as the proportion of young people in this country declines. Given the monumental task of recruitment, employment screening, and training new employees in the future, it will be more fiscally and administratively sound to attempt to concentrate upon limiting the potential and actual attrition of the veteran employee. As a result, a primary goal of the police agency of the future will be *retention,* not recruitment. In addition, the experience and knowledge of the veteran employee will probably be more crucial in the increasingly complex and litigious external environment of the future. In *Reinventing the Corporation* (Naisbitt & Aburdene, 1985:104), a private sector executive was quoted as saying: "The wisdom, judgment, and experience [of older workers] are invaluable to the corporation. They are a vital future manpower resource." Given the demographic trends of the future, the veteran law enforcement employee must also be recognized as a "vital future manpower resource" for the year 2000 and beyond.

Management Trend #3: The New Management Philosophy

When examining the organizational and leadership philosophy of most police agencies, it is generally recognized that the bureaucratic model and its autocratic leadership style remains the primary choice of many criminal justice managers (Swanson, Territo & Taylor, 1988:91). The ideas of Max Weber, Frederick W. Taylor, and other traditional theorists have continued to influence criminal justice management. It should be noted that, at the time of Weber and Taylor, organizations were almost exclusively white and male, and all organizations including those in law enforcement were operating in an environment where change was much less complex and dramatic. Weber's bureaucratic model and Taylor's "Scientific Management" were designed for an industrialized America where jobs were labor-intensive, the labor pool was young and seemingly inexhaustible, and employees generally looked and acted the same. As a result, management techniques were based upon compliance with extensive rules and regulations with little or no input or participation from employees. The autocratic "my way or the highway" management philosophy found little resistance in the earlier portion of this century.

America of the 1990s and beyond will not be so simple and undiversified. Employees of today and tomorrow will increasingly represent minority, female, or older portions of society. They will also be better educated than their early twentieth century counterparts. As society and the work place become more diversified, the versatility and practicality of an autocratic/nonparticipative style of management has become more apparent. The private sector has seen the limitations of autocratic/technocratic leadership, but American law enforcement has tenaciously held onto this more traditional management philosophy. In *Megatrends*, Naisbitt remarked that the leader of the future must be ". . . a facilitator, not an order giver" (p. 188). The autocratic model of most police managers will not be prepared to take on this facilitative role. As a result, it is unlikely that the more traditional forms of law enforcement management philosophies will remain intact in the future. Perhaps the greatest challenge to American police will not be new forms of crime but the ability of the forces to manage their internal issues and procedures.

Summary and Conclusions

As throughout history, the American police system will be influenced, both externally and internally, by the demographic trends of today and the future. In light of these changes, many of the present philosophies and operational policies of law enforcement agencies will gradually become less able to cope with a world that is even more complex and dynamic than the one that exists today. Our criminal justice system has often been accused of being slow to respond to change. In the future, this hesitancy to embrace change may be more damaging than in the past. In his book *Megatrends*, Naisbitt remarked that many cities, companies, and organizations could be likened to:

> dinosaurs waiting for the weather to change. This weather is not going to change. The very ground is shifting beneath us and what is called for is nothing less than a reconceptualization of our roles (p. 95).

Given the demographic trends and other forms of change discussed in this paper, the "reconceptualization" of the role of police management is vital to law enforcement's ability to meet the changing demands of crime and of its "new employees." Failure to do so will most certainly doom the system to the plight of the dinosaur.

References

Bennett, G. (1987). *Crimewarps: The Future of Crime in America.* Garden City, NY: Anchor Press/Doubleday.

Cole, G. (1985). *The American System of Criminal Justice* (5th ed.). Pacific Grove, CA: Brooks/Cole.

Del Pinal, J. (1988). "Hispanic Educational Attainment Highest Ever, Census Bureau Reports." *United States Department of Commerce News* (Report No. CB88-142, September 5). Washington, DC: Bureau of the Census.

Flanagan, T. & K. Jamieson (1988). *Sourcebook of Criminal Justice Statistics: 1987.* Washington, DC: U.S. Government Printing Office.

Hindelang, M., C. Dunn, L. Sutton & A. Aumick (1973). *Sourcebook of Criminal Justice Statistics: 1973.* Washington, DC: U.S. Government Printing Office.

Lindquist, J. & J. Duke (1987). "The Elderly Victim at Risk: Explaining the Fear-Victimization Paradox." In J. Sheley (ed.), *Exploring Crime: Readings in Criminology and Criminal Justice*, pp. 55-63. Belmont, CA: Wadsworth.

McCaghy, C. & S. Cernkovich (1987). *Crime in American Society* (2nd ed.). New York, NY: Macmillan.

McCord, R. & E. Wicker (1990). "Tomorrow's Challenge: Law Enforcement's Coming Challenge." *FBI Law Enforcement Bulletin*, 59,1:28-32.

Miller, L. (1988). "First Baby Boomers Reach Age 40, Census Bureau Reports." *United States Department of Commerce News* (Report No. CB88-53, April 8). Washington, DC: Bureau of the Census.

Naisbitt, J. (1982). *Megatrends: Ten New Directions Transforming Our Lives.* New York, NY: Warner Books.

Naisbitt, J. & P. Aburdene (1985). *Re-Inventing the Corporation: Transforming Your Job and Your Company for the New Information Society.* New York, NY: Warner Books.

_________ (1990). *Megatrends 2000: Ten New Directions for the 1990s.* New York, NY: William Morrow and Company.

Parisi, N., M. Gottfredson, M. Hindelang & T. Flanagan (1979). *Sourcebook of Criminal Justice Statistics: 1978.* Washington, DC: U.S. Government Printing Office.

Passell, J. (1986). "Immigration to the United States." Paper presented at the meeting of the Census Table, Washington, DC, August.

Spencer, G. (1989). "Black Population Projected to Increase 50 Percent by Year 2030, Census Bureau Reports." *United States Department of Commerce* (Report No. CB89-B.01, February 1). Washington, DC: Bureau of the Census.

Swanson, C., L. Territo & R. Taylor (1988). *Police Administration: Structures, Processes, and Behavior* (2nd ed.). New York, NY: Macmillan.

Tafoya, W. (1987). "Into the Future: A Look at the 21st Century." *Law Enforcement Technology,* (Sept/Oct): 16-20, 82-86.

Toffler, A. & H. Torrer (1990). "The Future of Law Enforcement: Dangerous and Different." *FBI Law Enforcement Bulletin,* 59,1.

Tomasi, L. (1989). "The Changing Face of Immigration." *State Government News,* 32,1:8- 1 0.

Trojanowicz, R. & D. Carter (1990). "The Changing Face of America." *FBI Law Enforcement Bulletin,* 59,1:6-12.

Wetrogen, S. (1988). "Three States Likely to Provide Half of U.S. Population Growth into the Next Century, Census Bureau Projects Show." *United States Department of Commerce News* (Report No. CB88-48. April 1). Washington, DC: Bureau of the Census.